Witness to Disintegration

Witness to Disintegration

❧

Provincial Life in the Last Year of the USSR

Walter L. Hixson

University Press of New England / Hanover & London

HOUSTON PUBLIC LIBRARY

UNIVERSITY PRESS OF NEW ENGLAND
publishes books under its own imprint and is the publisher for Brandeis University
Press, Brown University Press, University of Connecticut, Dartmouth College, Middlebury College Press, University of New Hampshire, University of Rhode Island,
Tufts University, University of Vermont, and Wesleyan University Press.

University Press of New England, Hanover, NH 03755
© 1993 by University Press of New England
Printed in the United States of America   5 4 3 2 1

LIBRARY OF CONGRESS CATALOGING-IN-PUBLICATION DATA

Hixson, Walter L.
    Witness to disintegration : provincial life in the last year of
the USSR / Walter L. Hixson.
        p.   cm.
    ISBN 0–87451–618–8
        1. Soviet Union—Description and travel—1970–1991.   2. Hixson,
Walter L.—Journeys—Soviet Union.   I. Title.
DK29.H59   1992
914.7′04854—dc20   92–56904
∞

To
all my friends in Kazan,
schastlivo ("happiness").

Contents

Preface

❧

THIS IS A BOOK about the ten months I spent in provincial Russia—from September 1990 until July 1991, just a month before the failed military coup that culminated the process of the disintegration of Soviet power.

I went to the USSR as a Fulbright scholar, a visiting lecturer assigned to teach at Kazan State University in the city of Kazan, the capital of the Tatar Autonomous Republic, located on the Volga River some 460 miles due east of Moscow. I was the first American to live and work for such an extended period in Kazan, a city of over a million people which before Mikhail Gorbachev's time had been closed to foreigners as a result of the presence of defense industries as well as traditional Soviet obsessions with secrecy and security.

Unlike most Westerners, who typically spend their time in the cosmopolitan centers of Moscow or St. Petersburg (formerly Leningrad), I passed most of my ten months in provincial Kazan. I did travel widely, however: to more than twenty cities, several villages, and through diverse regions and republics stretching thousands of miles from Siberia to the Caucasus.

What follows constitutes a memoir of sorts, one that offers a sense of what it was like for an eager but naïve Westerner to live day to day in the midst of what was then still known as the Union of Soviet Socialist Republics. Rather than write an academic book swarming with footnotes, I wanted to offer a personal account, one that I hope conveys a sense of what life was like at a pivotal time in

Soviet history—indeed, what life was like at the very *end* of Soviet history.

While this book is an account of my experiences with everyday life in provincial Russia and contains no formal thesis per se, I do present a wide range of anecdotes, events, and incidents that reflect the growing popularity of Western culture within the former USSR. I was repeatedly struck by the number of people who expressed uncritical fascination with the West and particularly with Western consumerism. The majority of Soviets I encountered were deeply embittered by the collapse of their own economic and social system and were eager to adopt Western models and concepts, although most of them knew very little about the realities of capitalist society. Because isolation and limited mobility have characterized their society, Soviets relied on often misleading images and symbols from television, films, music videos, and other sources in forming their perceptions about the West. Nonetheless, it is the quest for better housing, clothing, consumer goods, and leisure activities—for the good life, for the "American Dream" even—that is driving the current changes in the former USSR. We live in an age of rising expectations, fueled by the global revolution in international communications, which has penetrated even the venerable iron curtain. Coinciding with the collapse of the Soviet system, the mesmerizing images of Western capitalist culture began to win over the majority of Soviet citizens, especially the younger generation.

I intend to subject these impressions to further scrutiny as the focus of my future research on cold war history. It was my professional interest in East–West relations since 1945 that prompted me to undertake a prolonged stay in Russia in the first place. I had written a book, *George F. Kennan: Cold War Iconoclast* (1989), on the American diplomat who had designed the strategy to "contain" Soviet communism in the postwar period. By the time I had completed that project, the revolutionary changes flowing from Mikhail Gorbachev's policies of *perestroika* and *glasnost* had made the USSR, and cities like Kazan, more accessible to Westerners than ever before.

Although I had read a lot of books, articles, government documents, and policy papers about the cold war, I sensed that I could never understand a place like the Soviet Union, nor my own country's attitudes and policies toward it, unless I immersed myself in the rhythms of its everyday life. I was tired of merely *reading* about the USSR—I wanted to *experience* life in Russia.

My decision to spend a year in the USSR stemmed in part from the critique of social and cultural historians, who since the 1960s have changed the character of the historical profession by emphasizing the need to study history "from the bottom up." I share their fundamental argument that historical change emanates from the masses of people rather than from elites, or "from the top down." Elites such as a Gorbachev or a Ronald Reagan obviously play critical roles in historical evolution, yet I believe they come to power and effect change as a reflection of the deeper stirrings of a society. Thus, I concluded that the only way I could make sense of the dramatic changes underway in the Soviet Union, and how the United States should respond to them, was to immerse myself in that society, to view it from the bottom up.

Prolonged exposure to a foreign culture is particularly critical in a field such as diplomatic history, whose *raison d'être*, after all, is to analyze relations among nations. How can one really evaluate US policy toward a foreign country without understanding that country's culture and society, its own sense of history, its peoples' perceptions of their place in the world? Can anyone really be expected to make sense of the history of the cold war without having gained some direct experience with life in Russia?

The field of US diplomatic history has been criticized for a narrow, Washington-dominated approach to the history of American foreign policy. Some have called for the field to be renamed "international history" to encourage a broader analytical framework. There are many fine scholars in the field, yet too few of them venture beyond the Atlantic or Pacific oceans to experience a foreign culture firsthand. When many of my colleagues do go abroad, they typically stay only for a few days, secure in the comforts of their tourist hotels and officially sanctioned seminars. Moreover, it is highly uncommon for historians of US foreign policy to learn and use the language of another people.

Relatively few academics are willing to make the sacrifices that an extended stay in a foreign culture requires. For one thing, I had the advantage of being single, which made planning for a year abroad relatively simple. The rigors of "publish or perish," which have never been more real than they are today in academic life, represent another deterrent. A year abroad usually translates into a year of little progress on book and article manuscripts. Indeed, within only a few weeks of my return to the United States, one colleague told me that I was in danger of lagging behind on the academic treadmill as a result of my apparently wasted year abroad. He advised me to rush off to do research in some archive while I tried in vain to explain that I'd just spent a year in the most immense and revealing archive of all.

Quite beyond those sorts of pressures, living in a foreign country—even one more stable than the former USSR—is quite demanding.

Immersing myself in provincial Soviet society, I lived in my own apartments, bought what food could be found at my local store with rationing coupons, washed my laundry by hand, competed for space aboard mass transit, waited in long lines, took icy cold showers, fought the bureaucracy, went days without speaking or hearing English, lost twenty pounds, and even started smoking cigarettes (happily, I've stopped again) and drinking shots of vodka, both of which are routine activities for most Soviet males.

Determined to understand Soviet society "from the bottom up," I went native.

While I did deliver a regular course of lectures on US history in Kazan, my most interesting experiences came outside the classroom, interacting with people ranging from taxi drivers to factory workers, businessmen, hotel prostitutes, and members of the Soviet "Mafia."

It was, of course, a very difficult time to live in the Soviet Union. Severe shortages of food and clothing made 1991 the worst year in recent memory, though 1992 has since displaced it, and 1993 appears worse yet. Along with the economic collapse, however, political instability made for an especially uncertain atmosphere in the USSR in 1990–91. Everyone knew that the attempted right-wing coup, which finally occurred in August 1991, might happen at any time.

While everyday life in the USSR was often frustrating and sometimes downright frightening, the people who lived there ultimately made it all worthwhile. Soviets compensate for their daily hardships, the dearth of material things, and absence of recreational pastimes, with their *bol'shaia dusha*, their great spirit, or soul. Despite the mess their country was in, countless Soviets displayed an almost incredible generosity, great personal warmth, and sincerity about themselves and their society.

At the risk of seeming melodramatic, I've taken the precaution of changing the names of most, but not all, of those people whom I introduce in this book. Some of the things I write about here could put them in awkward situations in their home or workplace.

And then there's the matter of the KGB. The Dzerzhinsky statue may have been torn down and some files thrown open outside KGB headquarters in Moscow, but the *nomenklatura* (power elite) will take longer to dislodge in provincial regions such as Kazan. My caution stems from knowledge that the Kazan KGB did keep tabs on me by questioning my Soviet friends and associates.

Men from the ominous sounding "Black Lake"—the nickname for the Kazan KGB office, which derives from its location near a small lake in the city—suspected me of being a spy because I spoke Russian, though not fluently. "Why else would he have learned to speak Russian if he is not a spy?" they asked one of my friends. "What is it that he asks about? What does he want to know?" When some of my friends and acquaintances proved less than forthcoming, the KGB was not above threatening them.—"Do you want things to be difficult for you and your family?"

Needless to say, such activities represent everything that was wrong with the old Soviet Union. Now that the Soviets have decided to transport themselves down the capitalist road, we can only hope that the KGB and its sponsors will continue to be counted among the first ranks of the newly unemployed.

The observations and opinions I put forth in this book are strictly my own, though I would like to thank a number of people for their input. My close friend and translator Leonia Sidorov merits special mention for the countless hours in which he patiently discussed Soviet life with me. Alsue Facehanova, her husband Ravil, and their two lovable children, Icylu and Irat, have been close friends both in Kazan and in their new home in the United States. Alsue has corrected several of my misimpressions about life in the former USSR. My academic colleagues John Bushnell, Barbara Clements, David Kyvig, and Christine Worobec read drafts of the manuscript and saved me from embarrassing errors and ill-conceived remarks. Tom Mach provided invaluable research assistance as well as much-appreciated enthusiasm for the project. Journalist Mindy Fetterman made many useful suggestions.

I made some wonderful friends in the old USSR, and especially in Kazan, so it is only appropriate that I dedicate this book to that city and its residents. May they forgive me for the errors, misunderstandings, and harsh judgments I make, while at least crediting me with trying to understand them and their society.

Witness to Disintegration

CHAPTER ONE

American Boy, American Joy

MY FIRST QUESTION WAS: "Where the hell is Kazan?"

It was the summer of 1990 and I had just received word at Bryn Mawr College, where I was undergoing a second consecutive summer program of intensive study of Russian, that the Soviet government had placed me as a visiting Fulbright lecturer at Kazan State University in the city of Kazan. In my ignorance, I'd never heard of the university nor the city, though both were quite well known to specialists in the West.

In Washington, the Council for the International Exchange of Scholars, which had forwarded my nomination for a Fulbright exchange, awaited my decision. Would I accept the offer to become the first Fulbright scholar ever posted in Kazan, a city that had been closed to foreigners for years?

Of course I would. After calling Washington, I took up my study of Russian with renewed interest. I labored over my dialogues and listened to cassette tapes in my tiny dorm room and as I drove in my car. During study breaks I would walk down to the main hall in our Bryn Mawr dormitory and stare at the little circle on the map that said Kazan, which sat perched on a squiggly little black line labeled Volga R.

I first took up Russian in the summer of 1989 when I drove to Middlebury College, nestled in the bucolic Vermont countryside, to enroll in its highly regarded intensive foreign language school.

Middlebury takes itself very seriously. Every summer language student must sign a pledge not to speak English for nine weeks. If caught, you can be thrown out of the program.

No one strictly obeys the language pledge, of course. We first-year students especially spoke a lot of English, which we thought was quite understandable insofar as we didn't know any Russian. We did it mostly behind closed doors, like teenage boys smoking their first cigarettes, or while playing basketball in the gym on the far side of campus.

The Middlebury program works, however. While some people opted for sanity and quit after the first week—before they had even had time to master the formidable-looking Cyrillic alphabet—those of us who slogged our way through the nine-week program did indeed learn a lot of Russian.

When the summer program came to a merciful end, all of us— college undergraduates, graduate students, business executives, professors, and CIA analysts—convened for a vodka-laced celebration. This, too, I was to find, was appropriate training for my future stay in Russia.

By the time I left Middlebury, I could sling quite a few Russian words together. If allotted fifteen seconds, I could say things like: "Salt . . . to me . . . pass . . . could you maybe, please."

I could utter still more such phrases, and say them much faster, by the end of my second summer of language training at Bryn Mawr in suburban Philadelphia, home of another top-flight intensive language program.

Once again, I found myself surrounded by bright college students whose nimble, uncluttered young minds retained all the nuances of Russian grammar while I puzzled over daily homework assignments streaked with red ink.

All the work and the pounding that my ego took studying Russian turned out to be worthwhile. By the time I arrived in Moscow, I could speak and understand a fair amount of Russian. Moreover, I wasn't afraid to use the language, since that is what we had been compelled to do in the summer programs.

After spending only a few weeks in the USSR, I could carry on long conversations with Russian speakers, or at least those who were willing to tolerate my bad grammar, botched syntax, and frequent bouts of incoherent stammering. Even though I tested their patience and offended their ears, kindly Soviets often complimented my Russian, mostly, I think, out of disbelief that any American who didn't have to do so would bother to try to learn their complicated language.

Over the course of my ten months in the USSR, I would experience every variety of what one of my Middlebury teachers had once described (a bit excessively I thought) as "linguistic breakdown." But I took pride in communicating with people, especially on those rare occasions, after I'd spent several months in Russia, when I spoke with someone who didn't notice that I was a foreigner at all. Once, in a hotel in Central Asia, after I had been in the country for eight months, two East Germans and a Russian whom I had met in a lounge refused to believe I was an American even after I showed them my passport. "You speak perfect Russian," the Russian man finally said to me, "you must be with the CIA." After we talked a while longer, he realized that while my intonation had become quite good, my vocabulary and syntax still left a lot to be desired. I finally convinced them that I was indeed an American, which only strengthened their conviction that I was CIA.

Months before that, however, my first real test with the language came on my very first day in the USSR, seconds after I stepped from the Pan Am jet at Moscow's Sheremetievo International Airport—at 10 A.M. local time on September 26, 1990. I had to find out where my bags were being offloaded. I was more than a little anxious, since they contained all my possessions and the airport employees had taken up the disturbing habit of rifling luggage and selecting a few items for themselves. They apparently regarded it as a sort of airport employees' tax. The airport proletarians were sometimes so overwhelmed by the choices involved that they simply made off with entire suitcases. Thankfully, Western publicity and official American complaints had curbed the practice by the time I arrived.

As I scanned the terminal, I saw an Aeroflot employee nearby and decided to try out my Russian by asking him where our bags were. He did a slight double-take but then I could see in his eyes that . . . he understood me. And when he answered, I understood him!

According to the US–Soviet exchange agreement that had brought me to the USSR, I was to be met at the airport by a Soviet official as well as someone from the US Embassy, but I had been warned not to expect this. Indeed, I was to find that few things happened as they were supposed to in the disintegrating USSR, where contradictions and Catch-22's were to be taken in stride.

Finding myself very much alone in the Moscow airport, I asked another bystander how I could place a call to *Goskomobrazovanie*, the state Education Committee of the USSR, where there was a Soviet bureaucrat charged with making arrangements for me. The bystander not only told me but reached into his pocket to hand me the required two *kopeks* as he gestured toward a public phone on the wall. Months later I would have been surprised to find that the phone actually worked, but at this point I was still a naïve product of the West, where we expect things to work and to be fixed when they don't.

When I got through to *Goskomobrazovanie* and to the desk of Comrade Boris Volchkov, I told him who I was and that I had arrived at the airport.

"Well, so what?" he responded into the crackling receiver.

"Well, uh," I stammered, "what do I do next?"

"Go to the *gostinitsa Universityetskaia* [the University Hotel] and wait there," he commanded. "I'll get back to you." Click.

A young man whose name turned out to be Dan, a fresh-faced employee of the United States Information Agency, was standing nearby to meet some other arriving Americans, who were clearly more important than I. I chatted with him while he waited and asked if he knew how I might get to the *Universityetskaia*, located across a wide boulevard from the most prestigious institution of higher education in the USSR, Moscow State University.

"Yeah," he advised, pointing, "go into the duty-free shop over there and buy a carton of Marlboros. Give it to any taxi driver and he'll take you there."

The New Soviet Man had been replaced by the Marlboro Man and smoking was endemic, especially among males. At the time there was a devastating *defitsit* (shortage, deficit), which found the population waiting in line to purchase stringy pouch tobacco, that they would then roll up and smoke on sheets of newsprint torn out of *Pravda* or *Izvestia*.

A carton of Marlboros was like gold, just as young Dan had implied, and I soon became acquainted with a *taksist* named Vladimir as we sped toward the city center. It was the first of my countless rides, all of which I miraculously survived, in badly tuned, rusted out, bald-tired Soviet automobiles that invariably careened down potholed streets at warp speed.

While we rode, I violated Soviet law within my first hour in the country by accepting Vladimir's offer to change money. I gave him two one-dollar bills for 30 rubles. (By 1993 two dollars would bring over 400 rubles!) Disappointed at the meagerness of the transaction, Vladimir wanted me to change $100, which is a fortune in the USSR, but I explained to him that under the exchange agreement I was to receive 830 rubles immediately "upon arrival," so I only needed a few rubles to tide me over.

"Checking in" at the *Universityetskaia* was my introduction to Soviet bureaucracy. Rude hotel clerks directed me to the hotel "service bureau," where I waited eight hours with my luggage before Comrade Volchkov made good on his pledge to "get back to me."

Seemingly simple things like checking into a hotel could take all day in the USSR. Everything had to be done by the book and lots of papers shuffled, processed, and signed. No one wanted to be blamed for doing something wrong, no one was ever in a hurry, and no one worried about customer service—an alien concept.

When I finally received a room at the end of the day, I was exhausted and my stomach was still trying to cope with the barely cooked hot dogs, beet salad, and sickly sweet decaffeinated coffee that I had bought in the hotel buffet with Vladimir's rubles.

As I unpacked I turned on the television and watched a show called "50 on 50," which featured a young MC wearing a Pink Floyd T-shirt, and then no shirt at all, as he introduced Soviet rock groups, most of whom featured an attractive female lead singer wearing the tight mini skirt and patterned stockings ubiquitous among young Soviet women (much to the discomfit of the older generation). By the time I'd hung up a few of my clothes, the MC was interviewing the head of MTV, which had clearly inspired the Soviet program.

It was my first hint of the huge wave of Westernization sweeping across the Soviet Union, a phenomenon that explains the USSR's current almost uncritical fascination with virtually anything east of Berlin. From movies, to rock videos, to capitalist economics, the Soviets—and especially young Soviets—are going through a love affair with the West and particularly, or so it seemed to me, with the United States.

As I continued to watch the television, the next group, consisting of four attractive young women, sang a song that I would hear over and over again in the USSR and which I would later translate. It's called "American Boy" and its popularity attests to the ultimate dream of many young Soviet women—to leave the country with an American boyfriend.

> *(Chorus, sung in English)*
> American boy, American joy
> American boy for all this time
> American boy, I'll go away with you
> I'll go away with you,
> Moscow goodbye . . .
>
> *(in Russian)*
> We have no happiness in our private lives
> We come to no purpose in our years
> Somewhere my prince is across the border
> I wait for you, come fast to me
>
> *(Chorus)*
>
> I am a simple Russian girl
> I have never been outside the country
> Don't sleep in America, my boy
> Come and take me, that's all
> I will cry and laugh when I sit in your Mercedes.
> I will be swimming in riches.
>
> American boy, American joy . . .

Listening to "American Boy" on my first night in Moscow was an appropriate start to my Russian adventure. I knew that the USSR was a rapidly changing society, but after ingesting a lifetime of Western stereotypes about communist thought control I wasn't quite prepared to see scantily clad Slavs singing on national TV about the dream of emigrating with an American.

I mulled over these vivid first impressions deep into the night and got only a few hours of sleep before spending the next day hanging around the hotel trying to use my rudimentary command of Russian to obtain information. But no one could tell me how long I would stay at the *Universityetskaia* nor when I would go to Kazan. I tried to call my parents and tell them I had at least made it to Moscow only to discover that the hotel's international communications link was down. It took me a long time to adjust to these sorts of daily frustrations, but I had no choice. They were simply part of Soviet life.

It would still be a few days before I managed to call home, but on my third day in Moscow the *apparatchik* Volchkov finally called with the news that I would be going to Kazan on the overnight train.

"What do you think," I asked the administrator in the hotel's service bureau, whom I had gotten to know a little bit, "will they even be expecting me in Kazan?"

"Oh, no," she laughed, "I doubt that they know you will be coming. You see, our country is very disorganized. I'm very sorry, it's horrible."

I decided to at least see some of Moscow before I departed that evening. I'd been in the city once before, in 1987, for three days as part of a package tour led by Intourist, the official Soviet tourist agency now undergoing privatization. Intourist tours bear little resemblance to Soviet reality. Groups of cash-paying tourists are *always* met at the airport, never have to eat at buffets, glide about on air-conditioned autobuses, sleep in comfortable hotels, and generally are kept oblivious to the underside of everyday life.

I took a taxi to Red Square to revisit the stunning onion domes of St. Basil's Cathedral, across the square from the high, crenellated red brick walls of the Kremlin, the historic symbol of Soviet power. "There's where that crazy German landed his plane," laughed my *taksist*, Boria, smoking down to the filter one of the Marlboros I'd given him. He was pointing to the spot across the square where Mattias Rust, the young pilot who had risked his life to make aviation history before languishing several months in a Soviet jail, had set down his Cessna in May 1987.

From Red Square I had Boria let me out to stroll the Arbat, Moscow's historic pedestrian mall, which had been revitalized by the wave of free expression under *glasnost*. Artists and vendors lined both sides of the mall and quick-draw political cartoonists hawked outrageous portraits of Stalin with an exaggerated mustache, Khrushchev with a huge belly and bald dome, and Gorbachev with a highlighted purple birthmark. I marveled in the realization that such displays would have been unthinkable just a couple of years before.

As I strolled by Baskin Robbins, I craved an ice cream cone, but the queue outside stretched to St. Petersburg, as thousands of Soviets lined up for a taste of the West. I settled for bland Soviet vanilla in a cardboard cup, which I procured from a street vendor. Still hungry, I also sampled my first *shashlik*, tough meat skewered over an open flame, which looks much better than it tastes. (I once saw a Soviet dog turn down a piece of it, which really ought to tell you something.)

I returned to the *Universityetskaia* that afternoon, packed my bags, and waited until a man named Aleksandr arrived in a huge Intourist autobus that comfortably seated 100 persons but which, absurdly, was consuming all that deisel fuel just for me.

After we threaded our way through the always heavy Moscow traffic to the historic Kazan Station, I gave Aleksandr some packs of Marlboros as a tip and he found me a *nocil'shchik* (porter) to carry my bags to the train. The bowlegged worker wheeled the cart so quickly through the crowded train station that I barely had time to drink in the intoxicating scene: lights flashing on the schedule board; all manner of exotic looking people striding toward their berths on a busy Friday night; the smell of coal-fired trains in the air. I felt I was in another world in another era, and was tremendously excited.

The baggage handler carried all my bags and boxes of books into my two-person "deluxe" train compartment. After accepting his tip—a dollar and a pack of Marlboros—the burly porter leaned close and, from what I could gather, offered to sell me some dope. Only later did I read that the Kazan Station was a center of drug dealing and cheap prostitution. He didn't persist when I turned him down.

Just as the overnight train began to roll, and right on time as usual, my compartment mate, Oleg, a fiftyish, slick dark-haired businessman from Zelenedolsk, a Volga city located just west of Kazan, joined me. He turned out to be a very decent fellow. He was clearly well connected, as are most passengers who ride in the two-person deluxe railcars. Oleg was a factory administrator who had been privileged enough to travel to the West, including New York and San Francisco.

Oleg ate a sandwich and we shared tea across a table by the window, whose white curtains depicted a fire-breathing orange and blue Kazan dragon, one of the symbols of the Tatar Autonomous Republic into which I was traveling. After we had conducted a little chat of sorts (including lots of hand signals to combat linguistic breakdown), Oleg made his berth, laid down to read *Pravda*, and soon loud snores resonated through our compartment. His snoring combined with my unfamiliarity with sleeping on trains kept me tossing and turning on the narrow padded bench for several hours before I finally dropped off to the gentle pitch of our railcar.

When I awoke at seven, the conductor had already turned on the radio, which featured songs by Michael Jackson and Tina Turner. The conductor carried steaming teapots into each compartment. Oleg insisted that I eat some of his bread and meat, as I had brought along no food, and Russians are firm believers in a hearty breakfast, at which they'll consume most anything, including chunks of cold red meat and bread. It tasted pretty good, though.

I spent the final two hours of our trip staring out the window at the beautiful autumnal countryside of central Russia. Leaves were falling but the grass was still green between thick pine forests and muddy villages. Unshaven men in high black boots trudged down the village paths, sometimes accompanied by women with peasant scarves tied tightly around their heads against the morning chill. Trains whirred past on the opposite track while an occasional worker could be seen adjusting rail spikes with a long iron wrench.

As we rounded a bend into Zelenedolsk, we crossed the Volga River, which appeared wide, dark, and magnificent below a high suspension bridge, at whose entrance a solitary Soviet soldier stood in a tiny guardhouse, a bayoneted rifle gleaming at his side. He looked extremely bored.

Oleg got off the train after receiving my promise, one of the many I would find impossible to keep, to meet again sometime.

As the train started up, I wondered nervously if I would be met at the Kazan Station, as I had no names or telephone numbers in case I found myself alone again. But I had barely begun to collect my things after the train pulled in when Volodia, a casually dressed assistant to the vice rector at Kazan State University, appeared in my compartment to welcome me to Kazan. I spoke to him in Russian, which brought a raised eyebrow in response, but he was cordial and helped me off the train with my bags.

It was a bright and sunny Saturday morning and I quickly took in my first impressions of Kazan: the crumbling red brick train station, a concrete plaza and four sets of rusty tracks, a busy pedestrian bridge overhead. Ice cream and food vendors had assumed strategic locations and lots of colorfully dressed people milled about the yard.

As I walked to the waiting taxi with Volodia, we were joined by a woman with curly light brown hair and gobs of pink and blue facial makeup. She introduced herself as Tania Smolova and informed me that she was a Kazan State University history professor and the person primarily responsible for coordinating my exchange visit that year.

This, I realized, was a pivotal moment: I was meeting my "shepherd" for the year in Kazan. We shook hands. She spoke good English, much better than my Russian but still far from polished, and announced that the first stop would be to her home for some lunch, as I must be hungry.

A few minutes later our taxi pulled up at the entrance to Tania's five-story *khrushchevka*, a typical Soviet apartment complex built during the Khrushchev era. As we trudged into the crumbling apartment building, its dirty courtyard patrolled by poorly fed mongrel dogs, Tania informed me that I would be staying "temporarily" with her and her mother.

The hotel administrator in Moscow had been right after all: Tania added that no one in Kazan had known I was coming until they received a call from Moscow the night before.

Nothing had been arranged. I would be playing it by ear in provincial Russia.

CHAPTER TWO

Disarray, Disillusion, and the *Defitsit*

❧

FROM THE OUTSIDE, Soviet apartment buildings actually resemble the "projects" in American ghettoes. They are rusty, forbidding-looking highrise buildings with a lot of laundry hanging out to dry.

Inside, they are much tidier and more comfortable than you would expect. Once into Tania's apartment through the main door, which was attractively upholstered in padded leather attached with brass tacks, there was a tiny entrance hall, a closet, and a bathroom that contained no more than the bare essentials of toilet, bath, and sink. The hall fed into a small kitchen, which housed a groaning refrigerator, sink, half-size gas stove, cabinets, and a small white breakfast table with square stools pushed underneath. There was not enough room for more than one cook to operate, although as many as three people could slide in around the table.

Back out to the main door, the hall veered left past a small bedroom with a wardrobe and the two twin beds on which Tania and her mother would sleep. The living room—the last and largest of the rooms in the apartment—was to be my bedroom. Theirs was a typical two-room Soviet apartment and the fact that three people would be sharing it was not at all unusual by Soviet standards. In the previous generation there easily might have been two families, as many as seven or eight people, occupying the same space.

The living room contained a couch that folded out into a bed, several armchairs, a color television, and a piano, which Tania's mother sometimes played. Over a small writing table were some shelves, which housed Tania's history books and classic works of Russian literature by Pushkin, Tolstoy, and Dostoyevsky, as well as several English language volumes.

Over Tania's small work desk appeared one of those maudlin full-color prints of the martyred Jesus, blood dripping from the thorns around his head as he languished on the cross. "Yes," said Tania proudly, noticing my attention, "I believe in Jesus Christ."

Oddly, or so I thought until I noticed the same phenomenon occurring all over the USSR, an empty Marlboro box and a spent Coca-Cola can were prominently displayed on the living room shelves. The preservation of such items, which are of course unavailable in regular Soviet stores, reflected the widespread reverence of Western consumer culture in the USSR—what was trash in our society was a precious icon in theirs.

When we first arrived at the apartment, Tania's mother, Valentina Mikhailovna (all Soviets use a form of their father's name—in her case his name was Mikhail—as a patronymic, or middle name) met us at the door, wearing a faded brown and yellow print dress and a big smile. We proceeded to the living room where she had already laid out a feast on the coffee table. There were salads, canned ham (a rare treat), cheese (also very hard to come by), fish, paté, and soup, followed by meat and potatoes. They opened a bottle of champagne and, much to my amazement at 11:30 A.M., a bottle of vodka. "Isn't it a little early for that?" I asked. "Well, you know," Tania observed, smiling, "it's our tradition to drink vodka with meals."

Having decided to adopt the basic "when in Rome" approach, I managed to put down two shotglasses of the deadly clear liquid, as well as some champagne. I was already learning that the only means of surviving the repeated rounds of toasts at Soviet mealtime was to eat in quantity, including lots of fresh brown bread, which is a thousand times better than that found in American supermarkets.

The welcoming dinner was a relief from the awful food I had ingested at the *Universityetskaia* buffet. It also served as my introduction to the joys of the *stol*, or table. For Russians, a big dinner is much more than mere eating—it is a major social occasion that may be carried out for two, three, or even four and five hours. The eating proceeds by courses and is interspersed with frequent toasts and breaks for smoking (usually outside on tiny balconies) and often dancing to the tune of scratchy old records, called *plastinki*. Since the occasion begins with a vodka toast on an empty stomach, inhibitions fade fast and even people who were perfect strangers before can become friendly in no time. So it was with Tania, her mother, and me.

When we finally finished our get-acquainted feast, Tania and I left her mother to clean up and went out on my first tour of the city. Once an unimportant provincial town, Kazan mushroomed in size during World War II as a result of the forced relocation of factories to the east to prevent them from being taken over or destroyed by the Nazis. Since then the city of more than a million people, roughly evenly divided between Tatars and Russians, has served as both an educational and industrial center with sizable aircraft, chemical, engineering, food, leather, and fur processing industries. The city has several parks, a riverport that makes it the center of recreational activity on the Volga, a historic university, and a host of cultural facilities, including museums, a circus, a beautiful opera house built by German POW's after the war and modeled on the Bolshoi Theatre in Moscow, and sports and concert arenas.

For all of that Kazan is a fairly typical Soviet city: dirty by the standards of most of its American counterparts; filled, with some exceptions, with unimaginative concrete architecture and potholed streets that are a noisy, hazy maze of pedestrians, cars, buses, tramways, tracks, and trolleybuses connected to screeching overhead wires. The air was far from pure and the sun shone at best irregularly, especially of course during the cold winter when six or seven hours of daylight had to suffice.

I had yet to discover all of this that first day when Tania directed us out of their apartment complex and a hundred yards or so down the street to the public transportation stop on Karl Marx Street in *Sovetskaia Ploshchad* (Soviet Square). The streets in Kazan, as in every Soviet city I visited, were named for Marx, Lenin, Gorky— the usual litany of approved fathers of the revolution, all now largely discredited and their names removed from street signs.

After a short wait Tania and I took a trolleybus to the tourist centerpiece of Kazan, the white, high-walled Kremlin (the word means simply "fortress") overlooking the Kazanka River, a tributary that intersects with the Volga in Kazan.

The name Kazan is a Tatar word meaning "cauldron," perhaps

a reflection of the internal strife that produced frequent changes of khans, the name for Moslem rulers, in the Middle Ages. Established in the fifteenth century as a far Western outpost by the followers of Genghis Khan and his Mongol army, the khanate of Kazan became the world's northernmost outpost of Islam and was wholly independent of Russia until Ivan IV ("the Terrible") conquered Kazan in 1552.

Ivan IV had been so proud of subduing the Tatars, one of the largest ethnic minority groups in Russia, that he ordered the construction of St. Basil's Cathedral in Red Square in the same design as the orthodox church, which still sits in the center of the Kazan Kremlin, to commemorate the occasion. According to legend, the ruthless autocrat blinded the architect of St. Basil's so that never again could an equally beautiful structure be built. Kazan has its own legend, that Ivan chose the daughter of a local Tatar potentate to be his wife and when she refused he imprisoned her for life in the high Kremlin tower overlooking the river. In truth, Ivan IV was already married but, then again, taking a Tatar mistress was doubtless one of the prerogatives of being the tsar.

The history, if not the legends, are very much relevant to the current situation, as Tatars seeking greater autonomy have taken advantage of the disintegration of Soviet power to advocate real autonomy, if not outright independence, for the Tatar Autonomous Republic, of which Kazan is the capital (see Chapter 9). Living in Kazan, I was to get a real sense of the multiethnic character of the Soviet empire, which along with the economic collapse explains the disintegration of the USSR.

From the Kremlin we walked a kilometer or so downhill to the "Kazan State University in the name of Lenin," which was the official title of the place where I would work during the academic year. Founded in 1804, the university is renowned because of its famous students and administrators: the Russian mathematician, Lobachevsky, was once its rector and helped establish the university as an important center of scientific education, which it remains today. The most famous KSU student was one who never graduated but for whom the university is named, Vladimir Ulianov, who borrowed his revolutionary name, Lenin, from a Siberian River.

Lenin attended the university, but was expelled in 1887 for participating in student riots protesting the tsarist autocracy. Once the unchallenged demigod of Soviet history, Lenin was widely despised by the time I arrived in the USSR. KSU students liked to joke that he was thrown out of the university not because he was a revolutionary but simply because he was too dumb to go to college. Despite their derisive comments, the students congregated, when weather allowed, on the university's main square, under the bronze statue of the young, not yet balding, student Lenin, standing erect with studious demeanor, library books tucked under his right arm, ready to lead the country on to the glorious revolution.

There is also a classroom, preserved the way it was when Lenin studied there, and a university museum, which is thick with Lenin displays. How long these displays will last in the face of the widespread, though not quite universal, contempt for Lenin and his legacy is anybody's guess.

From the university, near the city center, Tania and I boarded a crowded tramway and rode three stops to the city's central art museum, which had on display the works of Constantine Vasiliev, a Russian who had been born in a village near Kazan. The paintings romanticized nature and bold, blue-eyed knights and blond-haired princesses from the Middle Ages. His work, which made Vasiliev one of the more popular artists of postwar Russia, showed more raw talent than subtle exposition, but Tania and I enjoyed the exhibition.

It was a crowded Saturday in the museum and I scrutinized the locals as well as the paintings. I discovered then that the people are great noticers and will do a lot of staring, particularly at someone whose clothing betrays foreign citizenship. They well know what can be found in Soviet stores—or, more accurately, what *cannot* be found—and my bluejean jacket and gleaming white Reeboks caught a lot of eyes. So did our speaking in English. About halfway through the art exhibition, I had attracted a small following of teenage girls, who giggled whenever I turned in their direction. It took a long time but I finally realized that the only way to avoid attracting notice was to dress like a Soviet, which meant leaving the Reeboks and the jean jacket at home.

After several days settling in, Tania and I returned to the university for a meeting with the Vice Rector for International Affairs, who was the administrator charged with coordinating my exchange. He welcomed me by presenting me with a US–Soviet friendship lapel pin. I reciprocated with a hardback copy of my book on the cold war diplomat George F. Kennan.

After some small talk I reminded the vice rector that I was supposed to receive 830 rubles "upon arrival," but had as yet gotten nothing, forcing me to change money with cab drivers and sponge off Tania and her mother. "I am sorry," he replied gravely, "but we have not yet received funding for you from Moscow. I will gladly give you some rubles out of my own pocket in the meantime."

I refused his offer, but I didn't like being broke even if there was nothing to buy. The vice rector was rambling on about the housing crisis in the Soviet Union, particularly acute in Kazan, and it suddenly dawned on me that he was explaining why I wouldn't be getting my own place to live anytime soon. After only three days in Kazan I was already frustrated over having no place to unpack my things, no work area, and no privacy.

For the next several days I wrestled with the money and housing problems. When I made a return visit to the vice rector, this time without Tania, and bluntly demanded money and housing of my own, he made a startling confession: he had no copy of the exchange agreement and had no idea just what the university's obligations to me were.

"You mean you really don't know why I'm here, what I'm supposed to do, or how much I'm supposed to be paid?" I asked, incredulous.

"Uh, yes, I know it's hard to believe," he replied, "but Moscow hasn't provided us with anything." I gave him my own copy of the exchange agreement and he promised to give me my ruble salary and housing as soon as he could. We shook hands and left in hearty agreement that things were moving along.

Finally, on my twelfth day in the Soviet Union, with Tania in the lead, we went to the university cashier's office three times, the International office twice, the accounting department and the vice rector's office once each, as well as another vice rector's office, and by the end of the day, I had finally received the 830 rubles that were due to me "upon arrival."

I had witnessed a lot of disorganization and nervous glances. At two of our stops, bureaucrats had upbraided Tania for bringing me along to witness Soviet inefficiency in person. Their greatest concern was not with the inefficient system, which everyone took for granted, but with my exposure to it.

Receiving my rationing coupons to buy food in Soviet food stores proved to be just as frustrating as trying to get paid. Every Soviet housing complex has an adjoining store but ever since the economic crisis set in under *perestroika*, their shelves had grown progressively more barren. When food, vodka, and wine did appear, they were available only with rationing coupons redeemed after a long wait in line. In Kazan the quantity of meat, butter, sugar, flour, and other foods that could be bought depended on family size, yet every person 21 or over had the right to buy two bottles of vodka and one bottle of wine per month.

University officials assured me that I, like everyone else, would be provided with food coupons, but for weeks nothing was done. The university needed to send a representative to the store itself to register me, but the woman whose job it was to do that never seemed to get around to it. I finally got tired of asking her.

Having learned that it didn't always pay to be nice in the USSR, I burst into the rector's office one afternoon and demanded to see him at once. When his secretary said he wasn't in and politely asked me what it was I wanted, I began raving in my accented Russian about not being able to buy food until a look of horror spread across her face and she got up and dashed into the adjoining office of the Vice Rector for Science, who later became a good friend. He received me, listened to my problem, apologized, and picked up the telephone. I received food coupons the next day.

Armed with my first paycheck and a set of thin paper rationing coupons, whose color changed every month, I went on my first Soviet shopping trip.

The food stores are even more depressing than Westerners imagine. They are invariably crowded with people but barren of goods. They smell like a combination of moldy cheese and very old dishrags. The female employees wear filthy white gowns and are harried and foul-tempered while the male workers, especially those who offload the cases of vodka, are frequently drunk. Soviet stores couldn't be avoided for certain basic necessities—vodka, milk, and butter (valued roughly in that order), but the best way to shop for food in the USSR was (and remains) through the main *rynok*, or private market.

The *rynok*, although clearly capitalist, predates *perestroika*. It has always been the place where those who can afford it, a distinct minority of the population, have gone to shop. The average

Soviet salary when I was there—before the hyperinflation that began in 1992—was about 300 rubles a month, which meant that normal workers could buy only one or two items at the *rynok* once or twice a month. I, on the other hand, with my monthly salary of 705 rubles (following the initial payment of 830 rubles) could afford to buy fresh meat, fruit, and vegetables almost every week.

The indoor-outdoor markets were colorful and plentiful places in every Soviet city I visited. They featured farmers and vendors from Central Asia and the Caucasus, people who grew their fruit and vegetables in the south and brought them to the northern cities to market. In Kazan, Kazakh and Uzbek men with large furry grey hats and Asiatic features weighed out the produce by the kilogram. Farm women stood over fresh-plucked chickens laid out on display tables while axe-wielding men wearing blood-spattered aprons hacked away on cattle carcasses on nearby stands. Pigs' heads dripping blood and rabbits shorn of their fur except for patches left on each hind leg, like a pair of high winter stockings, provided local color.

On my first visit to the bazaar, Tania's mother joined other women—and the shoppers were almost always women, of course—in bickering over the prices and quality of the meat and produce at the *rynok*. They would remove from the scales spotty vegetables or pieces of meat with too much bone on them. When I complimented Valentina Mikhailovna on her shopping skills, she replied "We have to study how to get the most for our money. We don't enjoy this haggling but we have to do it. *My privyki* ("We're used to it").

I was beginning to understand why bitterness and frustration accompanied the Soviets on every shopping trip. It was not merely the struggle to find and be able to afford to buy food, though that of course was pretty unsettling, but the whole sense that public order was collapsing as a result of the economic and political crisis that most disturbed Soviet citizens.

Psychologically, it was very difficult for them not only to struggle to get by every day, but to realize that the situation in their country was rapidly deteriorating and had been doing so for years. Their anxieties multiplied as they wondered just how bad it would get and when and where it would all end. Repression? Famine? Civil war? They didn't know. "This is our life," sighed one friend of mine in a typical refrain. "Who knows what it will be like tomorrow. Anything is possible with us."

Although the majority of Soviets I met were clearly anti-communist, they sometimes contradicted themselves with nostalgic reveries for the pre-*perestroika* days when the party bosses fulfilled five-year plans and made sure there was food on the local store shelves; when the buying power of the ruble meant something; and when only a very few items had to be rationed.

I found that many of the people who hated the system in 1990–91 blamed *perestroika*, not what had come before it. One university science professor recalled that in the first years of Gorbachev's power there had still been enough authority in the old system to keep the store shelves full. "Three or four years ago we had everything—meat, cheese, eggs, even frozen products—all of it was right there on the shelves," he told me in October 1990. The stores were so depressingly barren throughout my ten months in the USSR that I still have difficulty picturing what he was talking about. It seemed inconceivable to me, in the wake of my many trips to the empty stores, but I know from many Soviet friends that the shelves were in fact once well stocked.

It quickly became clear that the *defitsit*, or dearth of vital everyday goods needed by the populace, including food, vodka, clothes, and medicine, underlay the anger and despair that were mounting daily in Soviet society. As I added to my Russian vocabulary in those early weeks, I quickly picked up two new words: *uzhas* and *koshmar*, meaning "horrible" and "nightmare," words I heard uttered almost every day as Soviets described their lives.

I could see it all around me in Kazan as I toured the city on daily walks in my neighborhood and downtown around the university. In the city's main shopping area, Bauman Street, crowds of citizens would file into groceries, clothing stores, Soviet dime stores, pharmacies—and find nothing to buy. Every day there would be a long line in front of the *tabakanist*, as nicotine addicts stood waiting to buy their awful pouch tobacco. On the rare occasions when cheese came to the city, always at the same store near the city's main square, a monster queue would quickly form. To buy cheese, you would have to stand there half the day, which many people were willing to do.

The looks on people's faces betrayed their frustration. Soviets on the streets were not the grim and unsmiling automatons of the Western cold war stereotype, but neither were they chipper. They tended to look harried, put-upon, resigned, deeply troubled about the future.

The depth of the frustration became apparent to me on a blustery November afternoon when some friends gathered for a birthday party. A birthday is a major social or at least family occasion that requires a feast, plenty of booze, and frequently involves everyone drinking toasts until dawn.

I had arrived early on this particular occasion and the hosts were in the midst of preparing several fine dishes, having just come back from the local store. I found them in despair and turning crimson with embarrassment. "Oh, excuse us, please, Walter," said the woman, Venera, "but there's no bread. We've just been to the store and there's no bread. Oh, we are so ashamed."

I already understood that a meal without plenty of fresh bread on the table was as unthinkable as a party without vodka. I told Venera not to worry. I knew they were busy preparing the dinner but I had just passed a neighborhood store on my morning walk. I would go there and get some bread.

So I took a brisk fifteen-minute walk and arrived at the store, which did indeed have bread—and a queue stretching half a block out the door! As I stood in my first bread line, it occurred to me that I was doing something I'd only read about and lectured to my students when describing conditions in the Great Depression of the 1930s. The Soviets standing in front and in back of me passed the time complaining bitterly about the *crizis*, which was a venerable Soviet practice. At one point a middle-aged man, already drunk though it was not yet noon, tried to bull his way to the front *bez ocheredy* (without waiting in line). "You are guilty" (*vinovat*), shouted a comrade, waving his finger at the man, but an angry *babushka* went even further, grabbing the drunk by his collar and slinging him out of the line. The drunk staggered back and rocked on his feet while the woman cursed him vigorously, but he bided his time before forcing his way in ahead of an elderly man a few minutes later.

I myself could merely have found a tactful way of informing someone that I was an American and the Soviets would have brought me bread immediately, refusing to take any money and falling all over themselves with apologies and confessions of shame for the miserable state of their society. However, I was adhering to democratic principles at the time (an obsession I would later overcome) and waited in line more than an hour before arriving back at the party as a hero, two fresh loaves of brown bread tucked under my arm.

Bread lines occurred only rarely, but other staple products were constantly in *defitsit* under *perestroika*, all of which made Mikhail Gorbachev very unpopular. "He couldn't win an election for dogcatcher," I wrote my parents in my first letter home.

When I arrived, I had a pretty high opinion of Gorbachev. I thought that *glasnost* and *perestroika* had put the Soviet Union on the road to a reformed socialism, toward what the Czech reformer Alexander Dubček, who had been overthrown by the Soviet Red Army in the "Prague Spring" of 1968, had called "socialism with a human face."

As a cold war historian, I was even more impressed by Gorbachev's radical international reforms. He had unilaterally pulled out of Afghanistan and Eastern Europe, the latter of which paved the way for German reunification; had curbed Soviet support for third world revolutionaries; and had proposed to halt and reverse the nuclear weapons race, throwing the United States and Soviet military-industrial complexes into a tizzy.

I had not been expecting the man who had been decisive in bringing all of this about to be despised by the majority of the Soviet people. "Yes, he's done very good things in foreign policy," scores of Soviets would say to me, "but what has he done for *us*? We live worse now than we did five years ago." It was as simple as that.

Ironically, of course, it was Gorbachev's *glasnost* that had given people the right to condemn the party leadership and speak out about their frustrations. Had I lived in the USSR in 1984 instead of 1990, far fewer people would have felt free to complain before a visiting American. Only very rarely, and only on the most sensitive of subjects (an encounter with the KGB, for example), did I find Soviets who were reluctant to speak their minds. Indeed, they were so open that I found it as hard to imagine that they once were afraid to speak out as I did to believe that their store shelves were once almost full.

Back in the cold war days, or so I've been told, Soviets used to defend their society before Americans; now they defended *American* society before Americans, many of whom—and certainly this was true of me—were far more critical of their own country than the Soviets were. One had to be very tactful: I found that if I criticized the United States, or tried to say anything at all positive about the Soviet experience, people became angry and defensive.

All of this manifested itself on the seventy-third anniversary of the 1917 October Revolution, which used to be *the* major Soviet holiday. The one I celebrated with friends that year was the last of its kind. The holiday, which actually lasted for several days, began when red flags and Marx and Lenin banners and pennants were hung on building facades all around the city. The streets were cleaned, crosswalks painted, and fresh exhortations of support for *perestroika* and the working class, to which no one paid the slightest bit of attention, appeared on banners and billboards. People were very festive, mainly because they didn't have to go to work and could eat and drink a lot (the stores were always a little better stocked on the eve of holidays)—certainly not out of any genuine reverence for the revolution.

On the actual holiday itself in Kazan, Communist Party officials, union leaders, workers, and others gathered at "Freedom Square," one of the central squares of the city located between the magnificent white opera house and the central Lenin monument. One friend told me that workers were pressured and induced to attend, including receiving cash payments and time off work, in order to ensure that a good crowd showed up to honor Lenin and to carry banners reading "Defend the Ideas of October," "Perestroika— Continue the Great Works of Lenin," or simply "1917."

I had a look at the parade, complete with uniformed school-children and marching bands, then gathered with some new acquaintances in their apartment. All of my new friends derided the notion of celebrating the Revolution and laughed bitterly as we watched ceremonies on television after consuming a huge and delicious meal washed down, as always, with bottles of wine and vodka.

One man, call him Valery, a tall, thin, and bespectacled craftsman who chain-smoked filterless cigarettes when he could find them, expressed nothing but contempt for Gorbachev and *perestroika*, declaring that even the widely condemned Nikita Khrushchev had been a better leader. "And Brezhnev, even when he was bent over like this," continued Valery, hunching his shoulders and bending over like a decrepit old man, "saw to it that the stores were filled. And what do we have now? *Nichevo!* (nothing)!"

I asked him if he didn't credit Gorbachev for allowing the unprecedented civil liberties, including free speech. "Of course," he replied, "it's important that today you can say what you want and it's true that five years ago you could not. But what does that matter when we can't even find salt in our stores?"

As we talked, the nightly news program *Vremia* (The Times) appeared on television and we all hooted at the procession of goosestepping Soviet soldiers, rifles held erect, right arms flapping to the cadence, their heads turned reverently toward Gorbachev and the party leaders perched high atop the Kremlin mausoleum. The program reflected *glasnost*, however, as the announcers reported that a gunshot had been fired, in an apparent attempted assassination of Gorbachev, and a report from Leningrad (as it was then still known) not only acknowledged anti-communist protests, but allowed viewers to see a banner that read: "October 1917, Our National Tragedy." *Glasnost* or not, at the time I was amazed to see *that* on Soviet national television.

Inevitably, as the *defitsit* heightened tensions and eroded support for the government, people began to turn on one another and compete for the scarce commodities. "The *defitsit* is affecting the people, Valery's wife, Anna, told me. "There is more rudeness, competition, and betrayal, even among friends. It is very sad." The economic and political collapse threatened to erode unwritten but long-honored codes of mutual respect, comradely behavior, and the warmth and generosity characteristic of Soviets.

As the social order deteriorated, more and more Soviets sought means, many of them criminal, to beat the system, but the most venerable means to get ahead in Soviet society has always been through *blat*. *Blat* means influence, or "pull," and having it is almost essential, especially in hard times. Tania's mother had *blat*—she boasted that she never stood in line—and indeed I saw her march to the front on several occasions to receive her monthly allotment of vodka or wine or a kilogram of butter, whatever she needed.

Her *blat* apparently stemmed from her party membership, long-time residence in Kazan, and work as a doctor who had treated many patients, friends, and friends of friends. Although it took me a while to realize it, I, too, had *blat* simply as a result of my American citizenship. Working together with Tania's mother, we arranged for me to have the right to buy food *po blatu* (through blat) at a store normally reserved for World War II veterans, a store that usually had plentiful supplies of meat and that rare commodity, cheese.

One way to think about Soviet society is to envision 300 million people searching for *blat*, constantly calling in their chits and wielding their influence, all in an effort to get ahead. An oversimplification, to be sure, but not too much of one. Instead of working for and within the system, which they viewed as corrupt, people spent hours on the telephone, riding back and forth on public transport, doing favors for friends, all in anticipation of being rewarded themselves. They might be trying to accomplish something as mundane as getting an extra bottle of vodka for a dinner party, finding a decent pair of tennis shoes, a plane ticket, or getting a home appliance repaired. The system simply failed to provide these basic services and therefore people sought to meet their needs by going beyond it.

Much of this was done cheerfully and cynically, with all parties concerned fully aware of what was happening. But the search for *blat* inevitably found people using each other, taking advantage, aggressively pursuing their individual needs. It could get in the way of and sometimes destroy friendships. But *blat* is a way of life.

After a few weeks in Kazan I had made many new friends and come to understand the grim realities of everyday life. I had no regrets about coming, but still had no apartment, no place of my own to work, no teaching schedule at the university, and far less personal autonomy than I was accustomed to.

Worst of all, my relationship with my host family had begun to deteriorate. After little more than a month it got so bad that I brought to mind Ivan IV's conquest of Kazan in arriving at a nickname for my appointed shepherd, whom I now ungraciously called under my breath "Tania the Terrible."

CHAPTER THREE

Breaking with Tania

WHEN I FIRST GOT to know Tania and her mother, they went all out in grand Russian style. Hospitality is sacrosanct in Russian culture and Tania and Valentina Mikhailovna were determined not to disappoint.

They helped me get ensconced in Kazan, took me on tours, to shows, introduced me to people, fed me three huge meals of delicious homemade food every day, whether I wanted them or not. They insisted on doing everything, from cleaning up after me to hand-washing my clothes. They were full of smiles, toasts, plans, and endless conversation.

According to the unwritten rules of *blat*, of which I had only an imperfect understanding, I was obliged to reciprocate in full. The more lavishly they laid it on, the more I should provide in return. I understand all of this much better today, but at the time our relations fell victim to a yawning gap in cultural expectations.

Tania, who like me was in her mid-thirties, and her 64-year-old mother were Kazan natives. Tania had matriculated at the university, gaining a candidate's degree in history, which required defending a dissertation. Her father had taught in another department of the university but, an alcoholic, had died prematurely when he stepped in front of a train.

Although Tania was my official "shepherd" in Kazan, she was interested in far more than translating my lectures and helping me to get established at the university.

Tania had one thing on her mind and it was the same thing that tens of thousands of Soviets wanted: to find a way out of the country. If she could not leave for good, she wanted to get out for as long as could be arranged. Her destination of choice was the United States and her vehicle was me. She once told me she was sure that God had planned the whole thing that way in advance.

It was "American Boy, American Joy" all over again.

Tania and her mother, like a great many people whom I met in the USSR, were deeply frustrated with their lives. They wanted to live better and for Tania to have more opportunities to advance, both personally and professionally. In retrospect, it would have been surprising if they had not tried to use me to better their station in life.

The USSR in the midst of the *crizis* was a society of shortages, hoarding, the constant search for *blat*, and jealous competition among the citizenry for scarce goods. As an American, I carried considerable *blat* as a result of my possession of gifts, hard currency, and above all as a living symbol of consumer-rich Western society.

While I was trying to get away from all of that, to live as much like a provincial Soviet as I could, Tania and her mother instead looked upon me as the opportunity of a lifetime, one they could not afford to let slip away. Because Tania invested so much in our relationship, she became extremely jealous and controlling to a point that I found utterly intolerable. Ultimately I felt Tania and her mother were what the Soviets call *khitrye*—calculating, tricky people—who would stop at nothing to achieve their design.

At first I was more than willing to go along, out of appreciation for their boundless hospitality, but after a few weeks I began to feel controlled and exploited.

Warning bells sounded from the start when Tania began taking my arm during walks, handing me her bags to carry, and trying to kiss me goodnight on the lips.

I had no prejudice in principle against the idea of kissing women on the lips, but in the specific case of Tania there was no attraction.

When Tania wasn't working me, so it seemed, her mother would take up the slack. She insisted that I call her simply "Mama." "You need a mother in the Soviet Union and that's what I'll be," she said, adding that Valentina Mikhailovna was too long and formal an address for people living under the same roof. She did feel affection for me, and I for her, but selfish motives also underlay "Mama's" efforts to tie me into the family.

Scarcely a day went by that Tania and her mother didn't speak to me about arranging for Tania to come to the United States. "What about America," Tania would ask plaintively, "will you be able to arrange for me to pursue my historical work there? You know it is my lifelong dream to come to America."

I told Tania that I was eager to try to help her get an invitation to study history in the United States, possibly at my university. She was extremely gratified, though she could have cared less about studying history, and we drank a toast to those plans.

When we commuted to the university, Tania tried her best to keep a tight rein on me because of her almost desperate fear that some competitor would try "to take you away from me." She begged me to promise that I would never use anyone else but her as the translator of my lectures.

Over time Tania's fear and jealousy—coupled with my own determination to preserve my independence—began to destroy our relationship. Small events became major crises that ended with bitter arguments. One day, for example, an ex-student of Tania's dropped over, a very nice young Jewish woman named Eira, whose husband had dumped her with their small child to go play soccer in the Crimea. The three of us enjoyed tea, cakes, and conversation. As Eira prepared to leave, I presented her with a block of black mascara, one of the hundred or so such items I had crammed into one pocket of my suitcase for the express purpose of handing out as tokens of friendship.

No sooner had Eira left with a big, Maybelline-induced smile on her face than Tania demanded an explanation. "Do you also have some mascara for me? I don't have any, you know, and that girl has done nothing for you. Mama and I have done everything for you and yet you are giving your things away to strangers and not to us."

I was stunned. I had given Tania and her mother several gifts—including makeup, cigarettes, stockings, chewing gum, pins and badges, and some cash. I tried to explain to Tania that I wanted to parcel out my little gifts as tokens of friendship to as many people as possible, but Tania made it clear that she wanted *all* of them for herself.

It was, as I realized at the time, a very difficult situation for Tania and her mother. Tania cared a great deal about her appearance and, though she seemed to have ample supplies of makeup and a decent wardrobe, such things were hard to find in the midst of the *defitsit*. Seemingly inconsequential items such as a block of mascara or a tube of lipstick, especially those with Western labels, represented a cherished gift.

A couple of nights after the mascara incident, Tania, who continued to arrange a schedule of events for me, accompanied me to a dinner sponsored by a Tatar group. We sat with about twenty-five, mainly men, who delighted in the presence of a real live US citizen since most of them had never met one. We enjoyed good food and repeated rounds of vodka toasts. At the end of the night once again I took out some of the souvenirs I had brought along, including a Cleveland Indians baseball team key chain and an "Ohio Welcomes You" lapel button, and handed them out to my new friends. As usual, my little gifts elicited broad smiles of gleaming black, gold, and silver teeth.

On the way home, however, Tania once again upbraided me sharply. "You haven't given me a button like the one you gave to that man you only met tonight. I think you are very selfish," she said.

As I stayed up nights analyzing the situation, I realized that Tania's response was in part a result of her aggressive personality, about which many of our mutual acquaintances also commented, but she felt she was justified. The way things worked in provincial Soviet society, she and her mother had done a lot for me; I therefore owed them and only them the fruits of my *blat*. Why would I give things to other people who *had done nothing for me*?

As these sorts of pressures mounted, we experienced some strains sharing the tiny two-room flat. Forced to live together in their small apartments and communal homes, Soviets simply don't have Western notions of privacy and preserving individual space. There is in fact no Russian word that easily translates into our word "privacy." Russians are perfectly capable of hovering all over you for hours on end, asking lots of very personal questions, and refusing to understand how anyone could possibly object to such behavior.

Since private bedrooms are relatively rare, many Russians have no concept of a person's needing a room as a sanctuary. In our household, Tania's mother rose early in the morning and would burst into the living room, where I lay sleeping, in order to gain access to the adjoining balcony. There she would clang jars and cans in their storage space as she began to prepare the day's meals. It became apparent that sleep, too, was not nearly as sacrosanct as in the West. Soviets learn to roll over and sleep through a lot of noise. I tried without success to explain that I was used to a little more privacy, but kept waking up early to the sight of "Mama" passing though "my" room.

I also began to resent the extent to which Tania and her mother limited my mobility. They both worked, which ideally left me time to read, study Russian, or write my lectures at home. But if I took this option, I could not leave the apartment all day since they had the only keys to the front door and insisted that it was impossible to make copies because of the *defitsit*. The upshot was that when I went out, it tended to be with Tania, which I think was the idea all along.

After a few weeks of this, with no independent dwelling or place to work—and no teaching schedule—I was deeply frustrated. I had enjoyed meeting new friends, getting to know Kazan, and my skills in Russian had grown appreciably, but my deteriorating relationship with Tania had begun to overshadow everything else.

Spurred by my sometimes heated insistence, Tania herself at last solved the housing problem. She realized that I was reaching a breaking point, but tried to maintain some semblance of control by arranging for me to live in the apartment of some friends. She convinced the woman, Natalia, and her husband to sign a contract with the university turning their apartment over to me for the year for a generous monthly allotment of rubles. After six long weeks living in the tiny flat with Tania and her mother, I packed all my things into two taxis and moved to the Gorky region of the city, far from the city center and the university, but under the circumstances quite acceptable.

On our last night together I took Tania and her mother out to dinner at their favorite restaurant. We ate, danced, and toasted in the usual Soviet manner, but at one point they both began to cry.

Despite our difficulties, we had become very close in a short period of time. It had been very exciting for the three of us to get acquainted, bridge cultural barriers, and learn about each other's lives and societies. But my moving out also left Tania and her mother with a profound sense of loss. With my drive for independence culminating in the move to a new apartment, they felt their dreams about the West slipping away, too.

Tania, by this point, was driven to desperation. The next day at the university she took me aside and invited herself to my new apartment that evening. The last thing I wanted after what we'd been through was more contact. I was tired, I told her, and needed to get settled in before having visitors. As usual, she was insistent to the point of obstinance. "I just want to make sure everything is all right for you there. I won't stay long," she promised.

"Okay," I sighed.

Trying to play the role of a Russian host, I put together a dinner of meat and potatoes, which Tania and I ate together in my new one-room apartment.

"Walter," Tania told me as we sat back on the couch after eating, "I must tell you something. I think that I have fallen in love with you."

Aieeeee!

"Don't you find me attractive as a woman?" she asked, sliding closer. "You will, of course, choose one woman to be with for the year—you have human needs, after all—and you will not find a better woman than me."

I tried to turn Tania away tactfully, but all that came out were pathetic sounding phrases about not wanting to compromise our working relationship with an intimate one. This went on for several minutes.

At the time I still hadn't quite learned what would become clear over the course of the next several months in the USSR: most Soviets cannot take a hint. One must be direct to the point of bluntness or they will keep on coming when they want something. They respect straightforward talk and it's difficult to be too blunt. I don't mean to be critical, really, because their way is more direct than our repressed Victorian hinting rituals, but it does require a mental adjustment on the part of a Westerner.

It took a long time but I finally steered Tania out the door and accompanied her to the tram stop. As I walked back I reflected that she already had a lover (though she had put him on hold when I arrived). I did not believe that she really felt any love for me. Her confession of love and attempt to lure me into bed had simply represented a desperate attempt to cling to me. She thought that I was naïve about life in the USSR, which was true enough at the time, and that soon I would be grabbed up by another woman, to whom I would give all my little gifts and invite to America, instead of Tania. My presence and all that it represented about a better world had tantalized her and she could not bear to see it slipping away. So she played the only card she had left.

I found the whole situation depressing, though I was positively giddy about finally having my own place.

But I still had to work with Tania, which we managed to do throughout the first semester. Her lack of total command of English required long hours of preparation before each lecture, with me sitting much of the time while she flipped through the pages of her Russian-English dictionary. She did a good job of translating, however, and the lectures came off well.

But Tania was still clinging desperately. She would find me at the university and inform me that she had made plans to introduce me to a group of people, or had booked a talk for me at an institute, or that we were invited to a party at someone's flat.

When I began to meet other people, to receive my own invitations and arrange my own schedule, she became livid. "When you are invited someplace, you must always take me along," she told me. "It is the way we do things here."

By my second month in Kazan I had become friends with a number of people—a British linguist in the English Department, whom Tania didn't like, and a bright young physics professor, a Tatar named Ildar with whom I became close friends. Tania told me that Ildar was "insane" and that I should be wary of him.

Tania protested bitterly when I accepted an invitation to give a talk on the American higher education system before the English Department—the presence of so many English speakers made her nervous. "They are trying to take you away from me, I am sure," she said.

Tensions continued to grow but I felt trapped as long as Tania was my translator and official "shepherd" at the university. Our weekly session to prepare the next day's lecture had become the most excruciating part of my time in Kazan, however.

In late November one of our weekly meetings began badly when

Tania greeted me by demanding, "Where have you been lately? I have not seen you for three days. Have you started seeing a woman?"

"Tania," I replied, by this time learning to be blunt, "that is my business and not yours."

Tania took this as confirmation. "Humph. She must be a prostitute," Tania declared, "if you are already having relations with her so fast."

While I stood gawking at her, she continued to upbraid me before concluding with a threat. "If you don't start spending more time with me," she said, "I will take away your apartment."

"You'll what?" I asked, incredulous.

"Of course, I will take away your apartment. After all, I am the one who found it for you. If you are not spending any time with me, or doing anything for me, why should I allow you to stay there?"

"Tania," I said, "you can't do that. Natalia and Oleg have signed a contract with the university. Besides, you wouldn't do that after what we've been through finding me a place to live."

"Oh, yes, I will if you don't spend more time with me. Natalia is my friend and she will do as I say."

We proceeded to argue bitterly before stopping long enough to prepare the next day's lecture.

After that incident I resolved to see as little of Tania as possible, though I foolishly kept a promise—made long before in the midst of mealtime toasts—to spend New Year's Eve at her house. Welcoming in the New Year is *the* major Soviet holiday, much anticipated and planned for. The celebration begins about 9 P.M. on New Year's Eve with a table laid thick with all manner of delicious specialties. The evening accelerates with toasts and cheers at midnight, carries on into the night with gift-giving and more toasts and cheers, and *never* culminates before dawn the next day.

In most homes, a small New Year's tree, a *yolka*, is decorated and, especially where children are present, a man will dress up as "Father Frost," a fat white-bearded Santa Claus figure who hands out gifts, and a woman will be the "Snow Maiden," his female helper.

I joined Tania, her mother, Natalia, and Oleg—the couple who had given up their apartment for me—with great reluctance. But I had promised and Tania had pleaded that it would mean a year of bad luck for her, that her mother's heart would break, etc., if I didn't come. Besides, she had just undergone minor surgery herself and had not reiterated her threats with respect to the apartment recently.

Tania's mother laid a spectacular table with a cooked goose as the centerpiece and two homemade pies at the end. She even found as a complement to the vodka a couple of bottles of Pepsi, which she mixed with water in order to make enough to go around, and then poured into everyone's glass. We toasted and cheered when the New Year arrived, even as a pristine snow fell outside in honor of the holiday.

By midnight Oleg was well on the way to completely losing himself in a bottle—actually two bottles of vodka—that he personally consumed. As I later found out, he was a recovering alcoholic and prone to relapses. He soon became disgustingly drunk, bouncing off the walls, yelling at his wife, fondling Tania, slapping me on the back (I got off easy), and generally humiliating himself. Natalia was so angry and ashamed that she returned to her home on New Year's morning and told Oleg to move out.

None of this would have made a great deal of difference except that in his state of alcoholic depression Oleg decided to return to his former apartment, which is to say *my* apartment. As it happened, he showed up drunk a couple of nights later at 11 P.M. I had plans to leave early the next morning on a winter vacation to Volgograd, Ukraine, and Moscow.

I was quite surprised, and also had a visitor over that night, a young woman named Gulia whom I had begun to date, when Oleg appeared at the door, reeling and reeking of alcohol. He was on the third day of his vodka binge. He asked if he could come in and have a drink with me.

"Sorry, Oleg," I said, "but that wouldn't be comfortable right now (*neudobna*). It's late and as you know I'm leaving tomorrow. I also have a guest here."

"Oh, you've got a girl," he slobbered with a salacious grin. "We'll just sit in the kitchen and talk. I won't disturb you."

"No, Oleg, really, it's not a good time," I said. "Sorry." But when I started to shut the door Oleg put his shoulder into it, burst in past me, stumbled into the kitchen, and sat down at the table.

I cursed him energetically and told him to get out, but he wouldn't budge. As I contemplated violence, Oleg explained that he wanted me to give him my Sony portable shortwave radio, which he had admired on a previous visit. "I just want to show it to a guy, show him what the American has, you know," Oleg explained, wagging his watery, bloodshot eyes.

I refused to hand over my radio, of course, and finally got him out the door literally by dangling a bottle of vodka before his eyes and walking him step by step to the door, where I gave him the bottle, shoved him out, turned the lock, and fixed the chain. Later I felt a little guilty about fueling his binge, but at the time I didn't really care if he died of alcohol poisoning or stepped in front of a fast-moving trolleybus.

Gulia had stayed in the living room through it all, though Oleg had leered at her as he staggered out. I told her what had transpired and she agreed that it wouldn't be safe to leave my things in the apartment with Oleg on the make—he had a key to his own apartment, after all. And so, early the next morning, I collected my most valuable possessions and left them with my next door neighbors, whom I had gotten to know and trusted.

I left for my winter excursion the next day. The two weeks on the road between semesters gave me plenty of time to contemplate my situation in Kazan. Except for my relationship with Tania, I was having a fascinating experience. Now my apartment, so long awaited, was under siege, no doubt, I concluded, at Tania's instigation. I knew that she had been in touch with Oleg several times because he had called to cry over the phone and ask her how to get his wife to let him come back to her. I suspected that Tania, angry at me for putting distance between us, had fed him the suggestion to drop in on me as a means of reinforcing her threat to "take away my apartment."

I had finally passed through my appeasement phase with Tania. I thought I had been as patient and understanding as I could be and that I had tried much harder than Tania herself to bridge cultural barriers. I knew it would be a *cause célèbre* at the university, but nevertheless upon returning to Kazan two weeks later, I went straight to the vice rector and unloaded the whole story. When I finished he sighed and nodded his head. "I have long known that Tania is a poorly brought-up woman," he said. "Only last month she cursed me for not arranging for her to travel to your country. I am sorry, you should have told me of your problems much earlier." He approved my plans to "fire" Tania and find a new translator for my lectures. We decided it would be best if I took a new apartment and this time the university promptly found me one.

By now I had already established good contacts in the English Department (just as Tania had feared!), where I found a translator of my own. I proceeded from the rector's office to Tania's apartment, where I gave her some candy, cigarettes, money, color photographs of her family and friends that I'd had developed in Moscow, and some more dollars.

But then I told her the news. Tania and her mother screamed, begged, and cajoled, but my mind was made up.

Then they became desperate again. "Oleg said you had four girls in your apartment and that empty bottles were lying everywhere the night he came over," Tania averred. "How do you think it will look when we tell the university officials about your immoral behavior?"

"*Four* girls?" I asked in amazement.

"Yes, he said four: one in the living room and the three you tried to hide in the bathroom."

I stared at them a moment and then roared with laughter. I shook with laughter for several minutes, as the weeks of pent-up tension and the absurdity of the situation expressed themselves simultaneously. By the time I stopped I had begun for the first time to feel liberated from the emotionally exhausting situation that had plagued me since my arrival. I'd always felt that I'd displayed considerable empathy for Tania, but at that moment, as they informed me of the tale they'd manufactured to try to intimidate me into doing what they wanted, any sympathy I had felt for Tania and her mother vanished.

"We can also write to your university in Ohio about your immoral behavior," Tania's mother warned.

"Why stop with them?" I suggested, getting up. "Write to President Bush, he should be interested."

As I tried to leave the apartment, Tania and her mother literally attempted to block my exit. When I did finally bull my way out, Tania's mother followed me, crying hysterically and dropping to her knees on the concrete outside, begging me to come back. "You will kill her, can't you see she is dying," Tania screamed from the stairs above, but "Mama," a decent actress, was just being *khitrye*.

I walked away, badly shaken, and never went back. I encountered Tania a couple of times at the university, but only a few cold words passed between us.

Tania exacted revenge in what ways she could. When the second semester got underway, she prevented me from continuing to work with a group of bright Kazan State students who had faithfully attended my lectures the first semester, asking many good questions about US history and contemporary life. Tania arranged for her own seminar, which the students were required to attend, to be held at the same time as my lectures, thus taking the students down with her rather than allowing them to continue with the rare opportunity to work with a Western professor.

Later, a couple of Soviet friends suggested the possibility that Tania might have been KGB. She had, after all, tried very hard to regulate my behavior. However, for a variety of reasons— principally her complete lack of subtlety—I very much doubt it, though I am sure that the KGB questioned her about my activities.

The break with Tania cast a shadow over my whole visit to the Soviet Union. I hesitate to write about the unhappy experience now, but I do so because it revealed to me the desperation that many people felt in Soviet society as well as the powerful allure of the West, which in this case I symbolized. Fortunately, the overwhelming majority of people, unlike Tania, didn't allow that sense of desperation and their determination to gain access to the West to dominate our relations.

The tragic story of my failed relationship with my host family has a rather happier ending. That spring I heard that Tania received an invitation, partly as a result of some letters I had written for her, to spend several weeks as a visitor at Texas A & M University.

Her dream to visit the West had finally come true.

CHAPTER FOUR

The Rhythm of Provincial Life

ONCE I HAD liberated myself from Tania's household, I faced the daunting task of learning how to feed and take care of myself. With a minimum of traumatic episodes—and a lot of help from my friends—I not only got along pretty well, but obtained the experience I wanted of living more or less like a typical citizen of provincial Russia.

I did my best eating on those many occasions when I was invited as a guest in friends' homes, but I still had to purchase food in my local store with my monthly rationing coupons. I went to the local market for basic necessities like butter and *kolbasa*, decent sausage that comes in long rolls and is a staple of the Soviet diet. I also redeemed my coupons each month for one bottle of sweet Georgian wine and two bottles of vodka, which I usually presented when I arrived for dinner in people's homes. (Always bring something, at least flowers, when arriving as a guest in a Russian or Tatar home.)

In an effort to stock myself for frequent visits to private homes, I sometimes traded my flour and sugar coupons for extra bottles of vodka and wine. There was always a small group of dishevelled men lingering about the store trying to exchange their food coupons for more vodka. I usually fit right in.

Occasionally I would buy a chicken or some beef or pork at the *rynok* (downtown market), but I felt guilty about it when I reflected that most of my friends literally could not afford to do this since one whole chicken cost about one-sixth of the average monthly wage. When I ate at home alone I usually prepared a concoction of fried potatoes and onions, slices of *kolbasa*, bread, and some pickles on the side if I could find them from a street vendor. I had one precious bottle of ketchup to go with the potatoes as well as several jars of peanut butter that lasted until I introduced it to some of my neighbors, who had never heard of the stuff before but definitely liked it.

In the morning, I would usually have bread and sweet homemade jam, which friends gave me, along with tea. The favored tea was a fine black variety that came from India or Sri Lanka, but when that wasn't available, which was often, we drank the inferior Soviet tea. Often I would eat my only real meal of the day—*obed* (dinner)—in mid-afternoon. I began losing weight as I started to live more and more like a typical resident of Kazan.

When I first arrived in late September, only meat, butter, and a few other things were rationed, but over the next few months eggs, flour, macaroni, cookies, and then even housewares, soap, and clothing—in other words, virtually everything one needed to live—were added to the list.

The positive side of all this was that some things that began to be rationed appeared in the stores for the first time. I still recall my shock and delight when, after two months in the country, I first saw eggs on a store shelf and realized that I could actually buy them. They certainly didn't come in individually grooved cardboard containers but I, like everyone else, managed to carry them home in a plastic bag without breaking them.

I also remember entering my store one day in late fall, stopping dead, and gawking at a shelf that had colorful red and white packs of Bulgarian and Yugoslav cigarettes stacked neatly in a row. I had never seen anything but the loose pouch tobacco before in Kazan, though cigarettes were regularly available thereafter. The price, three to seven rubles a pack, was about ten times what it used to be, however.

When the rare items appeared on the store shelves, the hoarding would begin. People bought as much of a product as they could simply because they didn't know when, if ever, they would see it again. The rule was: if you see it, buy it, and in as great a quantity as possible.

The populace found all of this unnerving, of course. They realized the country was in the midst of a deep economic slide and no one knew where the bottom was. "Next we'll be rationing bread," they would snort. There was a lot of joking and laughing about the *defitsit*, too, but the humor was acid.

One never knew what would be available in the local store, which was the only place where rationing coupons could be redeemed. There was no such thing as shopping at the grocer of your choice in Kazan. It was merely your misfortune if your store happened to be in a bad location, or your store manager lacked *blat*, or your store employees were particularly corrupt and stole more than employees of other stores before the food reached the shelves. Food store employees were always the best-fed people in town—some even toted big Santa Claus bellies, though there are relatively few overweight people in Russia. In addition to the extra weight, store employees carried a lot of *blat* because of their access to food, which they could steal (they wouldn't think of their activity as theft; just taking advantage as anyone would do) and trade for other goods.

My particular store, located adjacent to my apartment complex in an outlying region of the city, was poorly supplied. For days there would be no butter, or meat, or vodka, then a shipment would arrive and gargantuan queues would form in minutes. There was no guarantee of success even after waiting in line, as supplies could run out before one got to the counter. Supplies were sometimes pathetically short because much of the commodity would be sold on the side by suppliers and truck drivers before it even got to the store. Then, after the store employees took their cut, there wasn't always that much left for the people.

During my first few months, I dutifully stood in line like everyone else, as part of my quest to see what it was really like to live as a provincial Soviet citizen. After a while I decided that I now knew all too well what it was like and that it was time to take up another venerable Soviet practice—wielding my *blat*.

By late winter I would merely walk into the store and find one of the white-gowned women workers with whom I had become friendly. They all knew who I was and invariably broke into big toothy smiles in my presence, apologized for the state of Soviet society, and begged me not to stand in line. "*Nam stydno*," they would say—"we're ashamed" (about conditions in their country) and would rush off and get me whatever I needed.

Using my *blat* was certainly much easier and less time consuming, but I often felt guilty and sometimes downright embarrassed. Once, when beef arrived in my store and huge lines quickly formed, one of the workers told me to wait at a spot at the end of a counter and she would bring me my two-kilogram monthly allotment. I heard her go over and in a loud voice (Soviets are rarely soft-spoken) tell the woman dispensing the beef to pull out some select cuts for the American. At that point several heads turned my way and people began to whisper and nod in my direction.

As I waited, a group of older persons joined me and I realized to my horror that the store worker had told me to stand where the elderly normally wait (they, along with war veterans, are allowed to move to the head of lines). One elderly woman looked at me sharply and said "What are you doing here, young man?," to which I could only reply, "Foreigner." She accepted this explanation with a nod as if to say, "Well, fair enough, there's no reason you should have to put up with our nonsense."

I got my meat and left, but didn't feel very good when I thought of the women clutching their squirming, whining little children. They stood interminably, holding onto their babies with very tired arms, and would get whatever cuts of meat the worker put her hands on, regardless of quality.

To wield *blat* properly, like insider trading on Wall Street, it helps to check your conscience at the door.

For all the limitations of quantity, quality, and selection, Soviet shoppers could not complain about prices until April 1, 1991, when Gorbachev and Finance Minister Valentin Pavlov—who later became one of the perpetrators of the ill-fated coup—removed state price subsidies, thereby doubling and tripling prices overnight. The announcement of this plan set off waves of bitter condemnation of an already unpopular Gorbachev and found people hoarding as much as they could before the price increases took effect.

I went out to get bread the day before the price increases and arrived five minutes prior to the end of lunch break. Sixty or seventy shoppers were massing outside, ready for the store to reopen for a last day of buying under the old state-subsidized prices. When the doors swung open, the people plunged in, pushing and shoving each other, old and young alike, even getting momentarily jammed together in the doorway like actors in the venerable comedy routine. I had long since ceased being horrified by such spectacles and resolutely pushed my own way through. Once inside people rushed to newly arrived stacks of canned fish and sardines and attacked them like piranhas, snatching can after can, elbowing their neighbors out of the way, and running madly to the next counter.

"All because of Gorbachev, all because of Gorbachev, he's guilty," declared one woman as she huffed her way out of the store, shaking her head in anger and dismay.

By May and June, near the end of my stay, the higher prices were beginning to increase supply ever so slightly. A few previously unseen goods such as packet soups, juice, baby food, and frozen fish sticks showed up and remained on the shelves because of their high price. One day, much to my amazement, I even found a roll of Velveeta-type cheese in my local store—and there wasn't even a line.

The price increases definitely hurt the Soviet consumer. The government offered "compensation"—a one-time pay increase, a handful of rubles—in a pathetic attempt to offset their impact, but if one redeemed all of her coupons at the local store, the cost would be somewhere between a third to a half of the average monthly salary.

I heard many complaints about high prices, with which Soviet consumers, accustomed to state food subsidies, had no previous experience. On one occasion, I picked up a gallon jug of juice and began to tote it home. Three strangers stopped me on the street to ask how much it cost, as if I must be some sort of fool or rich man for buying it. To my embarrassment, I hadn't even paid attention to the cost. Most Soviets could not afford to be so cavalier, like the old man I once saw throw a packet of instant soup back onto the shelf because of its high price—about 15 cents.

The situation was even worse regarding clothing, with the prices of some items more than quintupling. I heard many parents complain bitterly about the price and unavailability of children's clothing. Their kids would outgrow clothes, or shoes, and they simply couldn't find or afford to buy them new ones. It seemed to be the one thing that depressed people most. "You think it's for ourselves that we are upset," a neighbor once told me, "but it's not. It's because we think of our children and how they must live."

The most popular place to shop for clothing was the downtown *rynok*, especially on Sunday morning when huge crowds of people turned out no matter what the weather. The sellers would stand patiently side by side in long rows, holding their used but cleaned and pressed baby clothes, jackets, shirts, and tennis shoes while thousands of people strolled by, occasionally stopping to finger the merchandise and, if they were serious, to haggle over price. Most people, however, couldn't afford to buy—they only went to look. It was something to do.

For those who had money, however, the shopping was sometimes quite intense. Once I toured the *rynok* with two American students who were visiting from Moscow. They had made the mistake of taking off their jackets as the temperature rose. They got no peace as provincial Soviets, hungry for Western fashions and assuming that the coats were for sale since they were being held instead of worn, kept coming up, fondling their jackets, and asking "*skol'ko ctoit, skol'ko ctoit?*" (how much?). One of my friends, carrying a Japanese camera, received the same treatment until we gave up and went home.

The "buy on sight" mentality applied particularly to hard-to-find items of clothing. I recall telling a friend one day in late fall that I hadn't brought any gloves with me from the United States, having assumed I could buy them in Kazan, which was, after all, a fur-processing center. Horrified to find that I had no gloves, she rushed me out of the apartment and down to the *Univermag*, the "universal" department store, where we found exactly one pair of men's gloves. She grabbed them from the saleswoman's hands just as another man asked for them. She insisted that we buy them immediately.

"I don't even know if they fit," I protested.

"We'll make them fit," she said, and stalked off to the cashier. We paid for the gloves before returning to the original counter with a receipt to pick them up. It truly is hard for an American to understand the need for waiting in three lines when one should do, but the Soviets showed no sign of changing the notorious system while I was there. Everything is toted up by abacus, which doesn't speed the process. I saw a number of cash registers in the USSR, but they usually didn't work.

Once I had gotten outfitted with gloves and a pullover cap I thought I was set, but a friend insisted that my Italian-made high-top boots wouldn't be warm enough to get me through the winter.

"Here," he said, reaching into his closet, "have some dog fur." He proceeded to cut some of the fur—taken from a dog he'd found dead on the road—into the proper size and placed the fur into the sole of my boots. I thought he was crazy until I took the fur out and found that my feet were freezing in the 30-below weather. Thereafter, I put the dog fur back in my shoes, where it stayed until spring.

The April price increases affected not only clothing and food, but transportation costs as well. I remember arriving in Moscow after being away for two months, placing the usual five kopeks into the turnstile at the metro and wondering why it didn't spring open. Finally, an impatient commuter behind me said that the price had just tripled the day before, didn't I know anything?

The price increases didn't alleviate desperate overcrowding on public transport, especially at *chas pik*—rush hour—mainly because people had no choice but to ride it since taxi and private car rates had become exorbitant. On the other hand, more and more people rode public transport without taking out their books of tickets and passing them through ticket punches attached to the walls of buses and trams.

Riding *bes platno*, without paying, was on the increase by the time I left the country and, since there was very little enforcement and only a small fine as penalty, what was surprising was that so many retained their sense of community obligation and continued to pay at all. Much of the time it was simply too crowded on board to gain access to a ticket punch.

Soviet transportation, like third world transportation generally, was notoriously crowded and uneven, but Kazan was even worse because its swampy landscape made it impossible to dig an underground metro system, which was supposed to be provided in all Soviet cities of more than a million people.

Getting a seat on a bus, trolley, or tram was a luxury, especially for healthy males, who were expected to give up their seats for women, children, and the elderly. If one failed to do this, he was susceptible to the challenge: *"Kak vam ne stydno!"* ("Shame on you!").

I almost always passed my countless commuting hours on my feet, clinging to an overhead aluminum bar in unspeakably crowded conditions, bodies crammed tightly together, people pushing, shoving, shouting, pleading, and quite literally hanging out the doors. Foreign bodies and faces, mud and sweat, crotches, drunks, dogs, sick people, crying babies, bad breath, pickpockets, teenage delinquents, giggling girls, nasty elbow-throwing *babushkas*, people carrying everything from stinking fishing gear to mattresses—one can find anything, except comfort, on Soviet public transport.

Despite the uniformly dreadful conditions, the people have no choice except to fight for a place on public transport. I noticed that all Soviets—from pre-teens to septuagenarians—were sprinters. When they saw a bus or tram coming as they walked toward the stop, they sprinted and, if necessary, lunged and elbowed their way inside the closing door.

What impressed me most about all of this, however, was how relatively calm people kept, how they maintained some sense of comradery, that they were in this together and could not afford to turn on each other. They even managed to laugh about it. I never witnessed a truly nasty scene, even under the most appalling conditions of the type that I was sure would have driven Americans to bludgeon each other in large numbers.

Soviets would usually help each other by making a place for someone to stand or offering to hold things, sometimes even children, for one another. One could also receive grooming and other advice while aboard public transport. "Young man, your shirttail is hanging out," said one woman pointing at my midsection, making it clear that I should tuck it right in to preserve public order.

Given the conditions of public transport, the most fortunate people were obviously those who owned their own cars, a distinct minority of the population. My apartment complex, home to thousands of people, usually had only about thirty or forty cars parked outside. Automobiles, the ultimate *defitsit*, were virtually impossible to buy for rubles, though I was told a car could be bought right away on the black market for two hundred American dollars.

Gasoline was usually available, but long lines at the pumps were inevitable—far longer than the ones that drove Americans to shoot and run over each other during the 1973 OPEC oil embargo. Almost every Soviet driver I met, and virtually all were men since few women are trained to drive, was his own mechanic. Lack of spare parts forced them to be ingenious and they sometimes amazed me with their ability to make broken things work without the proper parts. But I saw a lot of flat tires under repair on the road—even though not all could afford the luxury of a spare—and also observed drivers leaning out their windows as they sped down the street, their left arms stretched out to swipe away at the rain with a handkerchief since they had no windshield wipers.

For all the risks and extra expense involved, car travel was by far the most efficient means of transport. Yellow taxis dotted the streets, but not nearly in sufficient numbers to meet demand. As a result, what we would call hitchhiking, taking a ride in a private car from someone you don't know, was an everyday mode of transport across the USSR.

This practice was much more dangerous for women than for men, but I myself spent many apprehensive nights, often alone in winter, catching a ride on a dark street late at night. Since it is an accepted mode of public transportation, one could usually count on getting a ride within ten or fifteen minutes at the most. Persons seeking a ride simply held out their right arm until a car stopped, at which point one was obliged to state a destination. The driver then either shook his head and drove off, meaning he wasn't going in that direction, or nodded approval. At the end of the ride, the passenger would hand the driver some cash, about five or six rubles in provincial cities by the time I left the USSR. If it wasn't enough, the driver would let you know, but he usually just took what he was given, often not bothering to count it.

I never had a serious problem riding in private cars in the USSR, though I did encounter drunks, but I heard horror stories of rapes, robberies, and occasional murders, including one of an Italian tourist in Volgograd a few weeks before I visited there. I knew a young woman, a beautiful Tatar girl who arrived at a Sunday afternoon birthday party, appearing radiant in a canary yellow dress, except that she was crying. It turned out she had gotten into a private car with two men who had sexually harassed her and had taken a gun out of the glove compartment and pointed it at her. Their goal had been limited to terrorizing her and they let her out eventually.

Like transportation, food, and shopping, Soviet communications facilities were another source of aggravation. Only about half the Kazan population had telephones in their homes so it was not always easy to get in touch with people. Without a personal telephone, and I had none, one was forced to use payphones on the street. There were plenty of these, but less than half worked, primarily because of vandalism. If the phone did work, you usually had to wait in line for your turn and then carry on your conversation while people hovered over your shoulder. I found it particularly disconcerting when a crowd of people stared impatiently while I spoke bad Russian into the receiver.

International calls could be placed from public facilities, but I preferred to operate out of friends' homes. They would order a call for me a day in advance and I usually, though not always, got through to the US in this way. On one occasion the call came through to a friend's home after I had left for the evening and my mother conducted a not very illuminating conversation with a friend of mine who knew only pidgin English.

The Soviet domestic and international telegraph system was quite efficient, however, and offered the most reliable means for getting in touch with someone outside one's city.

Domestic mail flowed securely in the USSR, but my mail to and from the United States took as long as two months to arrive, in part because the KGB felt compelled to tamper with it. I seriously considered taking my outgoing mail directly to the KGB office, the notorious "Black Lake," rather than to the post office. I thought I might walk in and ask them with a straight face if my bringing the mail directly to them might shave a week or two off the delivery time, but vetoed the plan as too provocative.

I received a lot of previously opened mail, which I sometimes showed to the secretary in the International office where it arrived. "You're not the first and not the last," she said, laughing. I lost a couple of Western magazines, especially colorful sports journals, to Soviet mail thieves. On one occasion someone had replaced the *Sporting News*, sent to me by a friend in Kentucky, with the funny pages from a German newspaper.

If the KGB bugged my apartment, they listened to a lot of mostly boring tape, but I did try a well-worn ploy to see if they were listening in. As the no doubt apocryphal story has it, Westerners know they are being monitored when they say something like, "Gosh, I wish I had some soap around here" and the next day a bar of soap somehow appears on the premises. I, on the other hand, many times said to my walls, "Gosh, I wish I had a way to do my laundry," but it never worked.

I had innocently brought with me several pairs of beige pants, which quickly became stained with the mud and grime that cakes Soviet streets. That, I discovered, is why Soviet men wear almost exclusively dark pants. I never saw a laundromat in the USSR, but a friend tried to help me get my things cleaned by going into the back doors of industrial cleaners and paying a worker a few rubles to do my things on the side. This worked a couple of times until on one occasion the worker wasn't there, another time the water wasn't running, and so on. Toting a huge bundle of clothes on public transport was no pleasure, especially when they couldn't be cleaned, so I gave up dealing with the industrial laundry.

In the end, as usual, the best solution was the most common one: I began to wash my own clothes by hand just as everyone else did. I'd never done that before, but I came to find it rather therapeutic, gritting my teeth and rubbing my dirty pants legs together, rinsing, wringing, and hanging my things out on the balcony clothesline. I borrowed an iron from the neighbors, but more often than not took up one of the young women in my building on her offer to iron for me. "A man should not be doing such work," they would say. After a few obligatory protests, I allowed them to iron my clothes, dispensing candy, color photographs of their families, and other knicknacks in return.

Washing myself was usually, but not always, easier to deal with than the laundry. Both apartments I lived in over the course of the year had running water and a bath with an automatic shower attachment. In the first, I had to turn on the water, trot into the kitchen and light a gas water heater, and then leave the water running when I was finished until I shut off the gas and the water cooled down.

I preferred this system because in my second apartment I had no control over the hot water, which was connected to the heating system. When they turned the heat off in May, I lost all hot water and had to accustom myself to icy cold showers. Sometimes, in both apartments, there would be no water at all, often for several hours. A large percentage of homes in Kazan, especially in the Tatar neighborhoods, had no indoor plumbing, however, so I couldn't feel too deprived.

The better I got to know provincial Soviet life, the more I came to appreciate how organized, efficient, and taken for granted are the comfortable lives of middle and upper class Americans. Although I had certain advantages over my Soviet friends—I was rich by their standards, had a great deal of *blat*, and could leave the country at any time—in a way I suffered more because the daily frustrations of Soviet life were all new to me. By their values, I was incredibly spoiled though I tried hard not to show it.

Over time, and it was a painfully slow process, I became accustomed to these frustrations, though I also grew quite cynical, which is to say Soviet, about them. As the following diary entry suggests, what I found most trying were the difficulties I encountered in attempting to accomplish the most routine everyday business.

Got up yesterday morning, had some tea and headed to the university. I went to the cashier's office for my pay, but the clerk sat knitting behind a sign that said "No money yet—come back after 1." One of my morning's aims denied. From there I went over to the International Office and tried to call Moscow about my appointment at Moscow State University next week, but for the second day in a row the phone lines were tied up all morning and I couldn't get through—two down. I then stopped off to see if they were going to post the announcement about my lecture course, as promised, but the secretary said there was a delay because all announcements had to be screened through another office, where the man in charge was out of town. Three down. I went to the post office to pick up a package sent to me, but forgot that the bureaucracy required me to bring my passport and write down my passport number in order to receive it. Four down. So I went back home. Three wasted hours and none of my morning's aims accomplished. All in all, a typical day in the USSR.

I now understood why the Soviets valued so highly the time they could spend together around the table, eating, drinking toasts, and getting away from it all. I also understood how Gorbachev had poisoned his own standing with the people during his first months in power when he sharply curtailed the production and distribution of alcohol and initiated the sharp price increases, all of which disrupted the routine around the *stol*. Entertaining without vodka, like eating without bread, was unthinkable.

As a foreign visitor, I had far more than my share of opportunities to be a guest in people's homes, which had both its benefits and negative features. Given the realities of the *defitsit*, I needed help from my friends in order to keep myself decently fed. Besides, I reveled in meeting different people in their homes, where I could get to know them, observe their family life, and learn about society. On the other hand, Soviets could be very insistent as well as very hospitable and I was often pressured to eat, drink, and go visiting more than I could manage. Having very little conception of private space, many of my friends couldn't seem to understand that I sometimes wanted to just stay home alone and read or listen to the English-language news on my shortwave radio.

While social drinking was hardly novel, I was not in the habit of drinking vodka, or anything else, straight, that is, without mixing it. However, there was little choice since wine was in *defitsit* (and designated a "woman's drink" in any event) and Soviets don't imbibe mixed drinks. ("Tell me, Walter, is it true," asked one friend, "that you Americans sometimes pour juice on top of your vodka? Why would you do that?")

When the drinking ritual began, I would drain my glass on the first toast in order to establish my masculine credentials, but thereafter tried to leave some vodka in it so that it could not be completely refilled. This gambit wasn't easy to get away with, as a chorus of Soviets would invariably waggle their fingers at me and say "*Do kontsa! do kontsa!*" ("Drink it to the end!") even as they held the bottle ready to pour me the next one.

Soviets learned how to drink in their teens and I met many people who could consume what I considered an excess of straight alcohol and show virtually no effect in their behavior. I met others who drank themselves silly, however, as well as a few teetotalers, though the latter were clearly outnumbered.

How much was drunk often depended on the occasion. Birthdays and major holidays such as the New Year required heavy drinking. I once attended a birthday party that began at 2 in the afternoon and continued until 2 in the morning. There were fourteen bottles of vodka lining the walls of their tiny freezer when I arrived. Twelve people drank them all by the end of the night, which, I was given to understand, was routine.

"How much do you usually drink?" I asked my friend, Maia, a petite, red-haired Russian whose twenty-sixth birthday we honored. "Oh, it depends. Sometimes three or four [shotglasses full], sometimes perhaps twenty. It will be closer to twenty tonight," she laughed.

"Isn't that a lot?" I asked.

"No, it's normal on a birthday or special occasion."

Sometimes I would attend these parties and wake up the next day with a mind-numbing hangover, swearing to myself that I would never do it again. While I walked around in a daze, all my Soviet friends, who had drunk much more, seemed to be fine and never complained about a hangover. They simply didn't admit the concept of a hangover into their mindsets. If they did feel a little fuzzy in the morning, they'd begin the day with another shot or two of vodka, or have some beer if it was available.

The Soviet version of a "six-pack to go" was no easy matter, however, as it required queuing up at a kiosk and getting watered-down tap beer poured into a plastic bag or a gallon jug provided by the consumer. Occasionally I would see a man running down the street, or panic-stricken on an autobus as he tried to keep his finger over a hole in a leaking plastic bag full of beer. The beer kiosks were most crowded about 8 A.M., when the serious alcoholics were ready to start their day with beer before working up to shots of vodka by afternoon.

Despair over the collapse of Soviet economic and political life exacerbates alcoholism, which has, of course, long been a major social problem in the USSR. Despite the shortage and higher price of alcohol, the sight of drunken men, and occasionally women, staggering down the street was not at all unusual in Soviet cities and villages. Public transportation facilities were sometimes deco-rated with multicolored vomit deposits left by drunken passengers. Soviet taxis, which always carry multiple customers, would often compel one to sit next to a reeking drunk.

I heard incredible tales, which might just be true, about desper-ate alcoholics who, when the vodka *defitsit* was at its height, drank medicines, automotive fluids that contained alcohol, and even ate pieces of bread soaked in shoe polish, all in order to get some al-cohol into their systems.

Throughout human history alcohol abuse has been fueled by tension, rapid change, and despair, all of which were in abundant supply in modern Soviet society, just as they were in nineteenth-century America, when the United States was, as one historian put it, an "alcoholic republic." Although alcoholism is a serious social problem in Russia, most drinkers, especially women, drink moderately. The average citizen will go several days without drinking. But when there's a gathering of family or friends and certainly on a special occasion, a few bottles will be on hand. When one bottle runs out, they would never think about saving the next one, even the last, for another celebration.

Rather than the occasional alcoholic debauch, most of my gatherings with Soviets consisted of moderate drinking and lots of pleasant conversation. I would meet people at the university and get acquainted with friends of friends.

In addition to bringing flowers and vodka, if I had any, I would usually take along a few Western magazines and color photographs of my family and homelife in the United States. My Soviet friends pored over the photographs with unbridled fascination, often flipping through the same pictures over and over.

Most of them expressed amazement when I showed photographs of my parents' 250-acre farm in Kentucky. Marina, a forty-five-year-old Russian woman, tried to come to grips with the concept of private property as I pointed out the boundaries of our farm in a landscape photograph. "You mean," she asked, pointing to the barbed wire fence that marked our line, "that if someone wants to pick mushrooms they can't come across a fence if it's not on their property?"

I explained that though most Americans didn't pick mushrooms, which is a sacred Russian pastime, my parents were friendly with their neighbors, who were welcome on their property. On the other hand, I added, they did post "no trespassing" signs to ward off strangers and people had every right to exclude outsiders from their property. Marina shook her head and didn't quite seem to find a place in her mind for the realities of capitalist society.

My friends would marvel at the size of my parents' kitchen and that each of them had a home office. "Think of it," they would say to one another, while staring at the photos, "entire rooms just for working—no one has to sleep in them." I usually didn't have the heart to explain that one of the bedrooms pictured was a spare that normally no one slept in.

Despite the disintegration of Soviet society and the harsh realities of the *defitsit*, people almost always managed to lay out an impressive spread of food or drink when I came calling. I encountered a warmth and generosity that somehow eclipsed what I was accustomed to at home.

My fondest memories of the USSR recall the many times I sat around the table with friends, having enjoyed a huge meal when I really needed one, and then settling in for long, laugh-filled evenings of conversation.

It's the thing I miss the most.

CHAPTER FIVE

White Russians, War Memorials, and Religious Revival

HAVING SURVIVED a sometimes harrowing first semester, I felt I deserved a vacation to start off the New Year.

The US–Soviet Fulbright exchange agreement provided grantees the right to travel in the USSR, either to give lectures at another educational institution or simply as tourists. Between semesters I chose to travel a circular route down the Volga River to Volgograd, then to Yalta and Kiev in Ukraine before returning to Kazan via Moscow.

When I first met with the vice rector, he pledged to arrange a winter excursion and ultimately that was done, but, like everything else in Soviet society, my trip neither came about easily nor proceeded smoothly.

When I approached one university official about my plans in early December, she grudgingly wrote down the cities I wanted to visit, but a couple of days later informed me that I couldn't stay in Soviet hotels for rubles, only for dollars.

There was a big difference. Soviet hotels are as expensive in dollars—they ranged from $200 to $400 a night in the best ones in Moscow to a minimum of about $80 in provincial cities—as they are inexpensive in rubles. According to my agreement, I had the express right, as a foreigner working in the country for an extended period, to travel and pay in rubles at the same rate charged to Soviet citizens. It was clearly stated in the exchange agreement, but I had to visit the rector himself to get this privilege respected. Things simply don't get done in the Soviet Union on the basis of one request.

I finally got a reservation for rubles in the Intourist Hotel in Volgograd, the first stop on my tour, and the university sent telegrams to tourist agencies in other cities, where arrangements were supposed to be made for my arrival. Though presumably things are now slowly changing, the USSR was, to say the least, not a country geared toward independent travel, especially on the part of Westerners.

Nevertheless, during my ten-month stay, I traveled thousands of miles and usually got my right to pay in rubles respected. But not always. The Soviets were desperate for foreign currency and did not let principle stand in the way of opportunism. With their country in the midst of a deep financial crisis, they meant to exploit us rich Americans for as many dollars as possible. More than once I showed a copy of the exchange agreement to a recalcitrant hotel administrator, only to have her say, in effect, "I don't care what your actual rights are, we won't let you stay here unless you part with your cash."

That did not happen in Volgograd, however, and my winter excursion got off to a good start. I had made considerable progress in Russian simply by speaking it every day in Kazan, but I was still shaky enough in the language that I wondered how well I would do traveling alone in strange cities where I knew no one.

Such anxieties were not alleviated when I almost missed my plane from Kazan because I failed to go through the wing of the building designed to serve foreigners. As a reforming police state, the USSR was still a society that segregated foreigners from the masses. Thus, every Soviet airport has a separate Intourist lounge and security clearance area for foreigners and one for Soviet citizens. They are in separate wings of the airport or in completely different buildings. The one for foreigners is usually clean, spacious, and comfortable; the one for citizens, dirty, desperately crowded, and hopelessly disorganized.

The Aeroflot (the state airline, also now undergoing privatization) personnel rushed me through the Intourist wing of the Kazan airport and I was the last person to board the jet for Volgograd. It was a cold January day and when I finally entered the passenger cabin scores of heads topped by fur hats turned to glare at the person responsible for the brief delay. (Amusingly, Soviets leave their warm hats perched atop their heads at all times in winter, even while sitting on an airplane.) Despite the rampant inefficiency in most sectors of Soviet society, I found that trains and planes almost always ran on time. In this respect, Aeroflot outperformed US airlines, though I understand the level of service has deteriorated since 1991.

When we landed in Volgograd, an industrial city of about one million residents, I caught a taxi to the hotel, showed my documentation, and checked in. Americans often came there to see the Stalingrad battlefields on summer Intourist tours, but the hotel personnel had seen very few Americans traveling alone in winter. I observed on their faces the curious stares I was to become quite familiar with in the USSR, looks that seemed to wonder if I wasn't some sort of Martian. But they were very accommodating.

A friend had offered me some motherly advice the day I left Kazan: "Walter, don't talk to strangers or go to anyone's home," she had said. "We have very many crazy people." I violated her warning on my first night in Volgograd, however, as I initiated conversation in the hotel dining room with a tall, greying Russian with big, piercing brown eyes. Let's call him Andrei.

He proved to be not only extraordinarily friendly, but a fascinating case study of contemporary Soviet attitudes. I spent most of my three days in Volgograd with him and his fiancée, Alla, and visited their home.

Andrei, like me in his mid-thirties, was a prototype of the new Russian: he was a businessman and uncritically pro-Western in his attitudes. He marketed onions and flowers as well as handcrafted souvenirs—mostly intricately carved and stained wooden locks that actually worked—that he made during the cold winter. In summer he led Intourist tours of the battlefields near his village outside Volgograd. He had plenty of rubles but also gained access to hard currency through his work with foreign tourists.

Andrei knew some English phrases, but refrained from learning more even though he worked with many English-speaking tourists. "You know why I never learned English?" he asked me. "The tourists wouldn't trust me, they'd think I was KGB. So it's better to use a translator."

Andrei was far less critical of Gorbachev than most Soviets I met.

"He gave us freedom. I like Gorbachev, it's just that he's not an economist," he observed. Nevertheless, his true love was the United States and the capitalist prosperity it represented. He tried his best to emulate a Western lifestyle despite the constraints of life in provincial Russia. He dressed stylishly in Western fashions given to him by tourists or bought for hard currency. He preferred gin to vodka, smoked only Western cigarettes, ate in the hotel dining room with its tourist menu most nights of the week, and generally eschewed a Soviet lifestyle. "I refuse to stand in line," he declared. "I simply won't live that way."

Andrei based his praise and platitudes for the United States on the country's material success as well as his contacts with American tourists. "Americans are the best people in the world," he told me. "I can understand them, they are the most like us. Germans, Italians . . . them I cannot understand. They want to tell you how to eat your food the right way. Americans don't care—it's just person-to-person right away."

I tried to temper Andrei's uncritical pro-US attitudes, explaining that ours was far from a perfect society, that we had many social problems, declining educational standards, violent and white-collar crime, but he would have none of it. He was not trying to flatter me, or get anything. Rather, his views were genuine and he enjoyed spending time with Americans, who were representatives of a culture he viewed as superior.

The only aspect of American life that seemed to bother Andrei was that we had given too many rights to African-Americans. "I can't stand *neeghars*," he said, using a crude version of the English "nigger," not the Russian for negro (*negre*). "I like white people," he continued, as if discussing the weather. "I can understand your, what is it called, Klan, yes, Klan, that wears the white hoods. I also think that *neeghars* should be kept separate."

I groped for a response to this straightforward expression of white supremacy and tried to explain that the United States had overcome slavery and overt repression to grant blacks equality under the law even as they continued to suffer from discrimination, unequal opportunity, police violence, and a host of social problems.

He was unimpressed, eyed me narrowly, and decided to test me on this point. "Walter, can you sit at the table with a *neeghar*, I mean sit down and have dinner with one?" Yes, I allowed, I could quite easily do so. "You could?" he asked, leaning forward in consternation. "You really could?"

I probed Andrei to try to understand his racism, but it seemed to be merely visceral, based on ignorance and very limited contact with blacks. Then he explained that he led a tour for a busload of African-Americans in the summer of 1988 "and they were all for what's his name, that Greek who ran for your president."

"Dukakis," I said.

"Yes, Dukakis, and I told them all I was for Bush and they all hissed at me, the whole busload except for two!"

"Why were you for Bush?"

"To me Bush is the greatest president."

When I pressed for his reasons, the best I could understand was that Bush is tall, white, and for Andrei symbolizes business and freedom.

In the end, we agreed to disagree. "You're a historian, you want to write books whereas I am a businessman," he explained, pouring another drink and offering cigarettes. "You can sit at the table with *neeghars* and I can't." He shrugged. "It's nothing. I respect you as a person and you respect me, that's all."

Although Andrei was the most straightforward racist I met in the USSR, many Soviets reflected confusion about racial issues in the United States. For years it had been a staple of Soviet propaganda that the United States discriminated against blacks and was a profoundly racist society. I would have understood had Soviets now concluded that the United States was *not* racist (since Soviet propaganda had told them that it was), but instead of drawing that conclusion I met many Soviets who had decided that the United States was indeed a racist society, but that that was a good thing! In other words, they hadn't rejected Soviet propaganda charging the United States with racism; they had rejected only the implication that racism was bad.

Thus, Andrei's racism wasn't an isolated example. Typical was the question once asked of me by a young Russian woman in Kazan. "Your negroes are lazy aren't they?" she asked. "That is, they don't want to work, right?"

On another occasion, several students approached me after I gave a university lecture on the civil rights movement, a lecture that, alas, apparently didn't come off. Was it true, they wanted to know, that black people now *ruled* the United States? Since the Soviet authorities had told them all their lives that African-Americans were powerless victims of racism, these Soviet youths had concluded that that was of course a lie and the real truth must be that blacks were *in charge* in the United States. They spoke of US whites as victims of arbitrary black authority.

"You have places in America where only white people are allowed to live and places where only negroes are allowed to live, right?" asked a man I met on another occasion in Moscow. "No," I said, "it used to be that way but it isn't now, at least not formally."

"That's too bad," his wife piped up. "I like it when the races are kept separate."

The word *negr* is also used by some Soviets to reflect a condition of degradation. While standing in line at the university one day, I ran into a nodding acquaintance, a middle-aged secretary who took me aside, apologized for the inefficiency, and invited me to her office for coffee. "I can't stand in line, I just can't do it," she said. "Let's have coffee and a smoke like white people, not stand here like *neeghars*."

While generally distressing, Soviet confusion over US race relations and the proper way to refer to African-Americans sometimes produced humorous results. As I ate one day at the US Embassy in Moscow, I met David, a young American black who had traveled all over the USSR in his work for the US Information Agency. Once, in the former Georgian republic, he related, he had had a long and interesting conversation with a Soviet man who spoke fluent English. They traded information about what life was really like in each of their countries.

Finally, after twenty or thirty minutes of conversation, the Georgian man said, "Now, let us turn to a new subject. You are a nigger. What is it like to be a nigger in America?"

"I told him," said David, laughing at the recollection, "that his English was really good . . . except for this one little word."

Having encountered more racism than I expected in the USSR, I asked some of my university friends, most of whom were not prejudiced, if they could explain the reasons for it. Some thought that Soviet racism stemmed from the fears and stereotypes that result from lack of exposure to persons with black skin. One university friend told me that African-Americans were so rare in the USSR in the 1950s that when he met a tall and robust American black, "I asked him 'Are you Paul Robeson?'" Robeson, the brilliant American actor, and a communist, was the only American black most Soviets had ever heard of.

"Perhaps part of the reason is the number of African students in the country," one university professor, Sergei, explained to me one day. "We went to those countries as their benefactor, with the attitude that we would give them aid and help them to develop their societies."

In other words, the USSR had adopted an attitude of *noblesse oblige*, of a superior nation helping an inferior one. "But then our people could see," Sergei continued, "that some of these students who came here to study in our universities wore Western fashions, blue jeans, and tennis shoes, things that our people could not get for themselves, and that some of them had hard currency. All of this was perhaps very upsetting to many people, that these supposedly inferior Africans might actually live better than we do." A Soviet woman who went out with an African, Sergei added, "would simply be scorned as a prostitute."

Sergei's wife, Lena, who sat with us at their kitchen table as we discussed racism, credited her husband with changing her own attitudes. "I used to consider that all were equal," she said, "Uzbeks, Jews, Tatars, Russians—except Africans. When one of them would sit next to me on a bus, I would feel very uncomfortable. Now I try not to feel that way because of my husband's influence."

Given widespread Soviet racism, it's no wonder that Soviet foreign policy has been an abject failure in Africa. Instead of winning their hearts and minds over to Moscow-led communism, Soviet attitudes send African students home detesting the USSR. I met one such student, named Robert, who was studying at a Soviet university in Central Asia. A native of Zimbabwe, he counted perfect British English among the five languages, including Russian, that he spoke. "I've encountered racism in many places," said Robert, who had traveled widely and was now in his third year in the USSR, "but nothing like in this place. I will be walking down the street and they will yell at me from cars, call me 'chocolate,' unbelievable things."

As a result of these encounters, by the time I met Andrei in Volgograd I was already somewhat inured to Soviet racism. I gave up trying to alter his views on the subject but still found him intriguing, a provincial white Russian chauvinist who struggled to construct an alternative lifestyle for himself even as he meticulously carved tiny wooden locks that symbolized the constraints he felt in Soviet society.

We agreed to meet again for dinner and he promised to bring Alla, his fiancée. She appeared with him the next night, tall, dark-haired, and attractive, wearing a stylish red pullover dress and gold jewelry. She smiled nicely and deferred to the men throughout the conversation, though she, unlike Andrei, noticed that I didn't understand every word of their Russian. Andrei was oblivious, even when I repeatedly asked for clarification, captivated as he was by his own speech.

I insisted on buying dinner and they insisted on giving me a tour of the battlefields near their village the next day, my last in Volgograd. I agreed and Andrei arrived with Pavil, a quiet but friendly neighbor who had a red, Italian-made jeep. We took the highway out of the city and then navigated narrow, potholed streets to their village of 3,000, which had been held by the Nazis during the war. Ironically, the village has been inhabited by Volga Germans, a tiny and often persecuted minority, for centuries.

Andrei pointed to sights along the way and explained that most families have relatives who died in the war. Bomb casings, shells, revolvers, canteens, helmets, and other wartime paraphernalia can still be found after the spring rains. He said that two neighborhood boys were killed only a couple of years ago when they uncovered and set off an unexploded World War II shell.

The village was tiny—it had only one store—but apartments were larger than in the city and children romped in the clean air, the boys playing hockey with crude sticks on smooth iced surfaces. After our tour we sat in their large living room while Alla served sautéed mushrooms and onions, which were delicious and went down well with lemon vodka and cigarettes.

Andrei showed me his handicrafts and some photographs, including partially nude shots of a Canadian woman with whom he had had an affair and who had bought him some clothes a couple of years before. Alla, sitting alongside, didn't seem to mind. They are both divorced and each has a child who lives with the other parent. "We are in love," Andrei told me. "I can't stand to be without her for more than a few hours." They planned to marry in the spring and said I would have to come down from Kazan for the occasion.

I took some photographs of them outside in the cold dusk air, mounds of snow in the background along a brown rail fence, and we piled into Pavil's jeep for the return trip to the hotel. They insisted that we again eat together in the hotel and, though I was tired and had to get up very early for a flight, I couldn't turn them down. Alla wore the same red dress, Andrei spoke at length, and I grew weary.

Finally I pled fatigue but before we parted I directed Andrei to the small storage room adjacent to the dining hall, little more than a closet, that housed Western cigarettes and alcohol for hard currency only. I selected a bottle of gin and told Andrei I wanted to buy it for him, even at the outrageous price of $33. "No, Walter, it is too expensive, I beg you do not do this. When we are friends you don't have to buy me things, I beg you."

I was uncomfortable even though his response was a refreshing change from my experiences with Tania over material possessions. I understood that Andrei wanted to stand alone and that it hurt his pride to be dependent on foreigners, but I bought him the gin and some bottles of orange drink that he liked to mix with his Western cocktails. I gave the clerk a $50 traveler's check, which Andrei noticed. "Ah, very convenient for you, but bad for me. I cannot accept them from tourists or the KGB will be after me."

"Yes, they'd want part of it wouldn't they?" I said.

"No," he replied with a smile, "they'd want *all* of it and would put me in jail."

I thanked them for their company and we said goodbye. "Come to our wedding," Andrei reminded me, though I never got an invitation, "and we'll find you a girl, a good clean girl." He winked and was gone.

I didn't spend all my time in Volgograd with Andrei. My reason for choosing the city as the first stop on my tour was to visit the memorial to the epic battle of World War II, or the Great Patriotic War as the Soviets call it. The Soviet victory, at horrific cost, marked the turning point of the war in the winter of 1943 and ensured the eventual defeat of Hitler.

I stopped first at the war museum, a modern structure adjacent to a massive brick building with all its windows blown out and whole sections missing as a result of artillery blasts. Preserved just as it stood at war's end, it is an impressive remnant, especially so when one considers that the entire city had appeared in the same grisly state. The Germans rained a million bombs on the city, destroying 41,685 of 48,190 existing buildings.

Inside the museum, a striking circular panorama composed of paintings and three-dimensional mannequins and artifacts recreates the battlefield. A young, conservatively dressed tour guide spoke in rapid monotone and I soon wandered away from the group of Soviet tourists, down to the first floor displays of shells, monuments, medals, and propaganda posters. Statues and paintings depicted the battle's generals and heroes, including a life-size painting of Stalin, one of the few such memorials to the brutal dictator still on display in the USSR. Memory of Stalin was impossible to ignore, however, insofar as the city and battle had been named for him until Khrushchev ordered the city's name changed to Volgograd in 1961 as part of the deStalinization campaign.

The centerpiece of the Stalingrad battlefield memorial is the stunning *Mamayev Kurgan*, or "Motherland" monument, created by the famous Soviet sculptor Vuchetich, which sits high atop a hill at the center of the memorial complex. Despite the cold and the fog that partially obscured my view of the towering figure, it was a moving memorial. The young mother holds a sword to the sky, her robes flailing in the wind, eyes wide and mouth agape with a scream that captures both the agony of war and the exaltation of victory.

Below, the hill cascades past a series of statues depicting the horror of modern warfare: mothers clinging to dead soldiers; soldiers carrying wounded or dead comrades, wall carvings and monuments to individual heroes. I joined a smattering of tourists in throwing a few coins into the snow-filled basins, where the fountains would sparkle next to bright flowerbeds in springtime.

Before leaving I entered the Soldier's Hall of Glory, a large domed structure with gleaming slate floors and golden-tiled walls etched with the names of the tens of thousands of soldiers who perished in the battle. Some new names, in off color, appeared at the bottom of some lists and I heard a bystander explaining to his son that their deaths in the struggle had only recently become known.

In the dome's center a thirty-foot ceramic hand protrudes from the floor, gripping at its apex a torch with the eternal flame that burns in memorial. Fresh flowers had been placed all around it. Four soldiers stood on their marks, rifles at their sides, in rigid attention as the few tourists filed through.

War memorials exist in every city, and young couples still honor the war dead by placing wreaths around them on their wedding days, in somber recognition for the sacrifice made so that new generations could live. They are not all as moving as the *Mamayev Kurgan* or the *Piskarevka* memorial cemetery in St. Petersburg, whose huge burial mounds mark the mass graves of more than half a million Leningraders who died in the 900-day Nazi siege of the city. (More Soviets died in the siege of Leningrad alone than all British and American losses in all of World War II.) When my mother, who knew nothing about it before, visited *Piskarevka* in the spring, she broke into tears in the face of perhaps the most overwhelming war memorial in the world.

Because of their direct experience, the Soviets know much more about the horrors of modern warfare than Americans, who have never suffered the consequences of an all-out invasion or aerial bombardment, the distant Pearl Harbor excepted.

Soviet reverence for the war dead and their nation's suffering is genuine, but the memorials long served another purpose as well. Victory in the war legitimized the Soviet regime and even legitimized Stalin, so that even today he is revered by many despite his paranoid brutality and perversion of socialism.

But generations pass, memories of the war fade, and despite the monuments in every Soviet city by the 1990s it was clear that the war could no longer serve to legitimate the regime. Even on May 9, Victory Day, the occasion when war veterans, both men and women, gathered outside Moscow's Bolshoi Theater, wearing their ribbons and chests full of medals, I saw signs of fading memories of the war. Few ordinary citizens joined the war veterans and almost all of those present were more than fifty years old. "My generation has no interest in May 9," one student told a visiting American.

Recalling Churchill's exhortative ditty to push the war to its conclusion—"From Malta to Yalta, we shall not faltah"—I left Volgograd very early in the morning for a flight to Simferopol, on the

Crimean peninsula, and a two-hour bus trip to the historic coastal resort city of Yalta.

I was following a nostalgic path of Soviet wartime history as well as seeking a warmer climate for a brief respite from the Russian winter. I managed by showing my copy of the US–Soviet agreement to check into the towering Yalta Intourist Hotel for rubles, though the administrator admonished me that I should have brought a letter from the rector at Kazan State, something that I had not been told in Kazan.

The hotel normally caters to foreigners, but they were eschewing the USSR in its troubled times. Besides, it was winter and too cold to swim in the Black Sea, Yalta's main attraction. The hotel was filled with Soviets, strolling about in their nylon sports outfits and cheap tennis shoes, stopping to gaze admiringly into the display windows of the hotel's hard currency gift shop. The women held hands or walked arm-in-arm and the men, too, casually wrapped their arms around each other's shoulders.

After catching up on sleep the first night, I joined an Intourist tour of the Livadia Palace, site of the historic February 1945 meeting between Roosevelt, Churchill, and Stalin to plan the postwar order. Yalta marked the highpoint of the Grand Alliance as exaltation over imminent victory obscured the gulf between East and West that within a year's time would replace compromise with cold war.

Erected in 1921, Livadia is a beautiful white castle high on a cliff above the dark sea, surrounded by gardens and monuments. I toured the interior and saw contemporary photographs and press clippings from around the world celebrating the historic summit. An electronic wall map with flashing red lights highlighted the battlefield situation in February 1945. In the main conference room three folders symbolizing the final Yalta accords reposed on a sleek conference table. Outside, on the fine columned veranda, three empty chairs represented the site, captured in a famous photograph, where the Big Three sat smiling (or as close as Stalin and Churchill could come to it—FDR never had a problem). Stalin had made Roosevelt, who had only two months to live, travel halfway around the world for the conference, but at least had had the grace to give the disabled president a large marbled room on Livadia's first floor as his sleeping quarters. The next day I toured the Alupka

Palace, also overlooking the sea just outside of Yalta, where Churchill and his entourage had stayed.

Yalta, of course, is in no way a typical Russian city. Its stone buildings, cottages, and hillside dachas invoke the ambience of pre-revolutionary Russia when the aristocracy reigned. Even today its pebbled beaches, good restaurants, and twenty-nine sanatoria preserve the town's resort character. The Chekhov Museum, which occupies the great dramatist's summer home where he wrote *The Cherry Orchard* and other classics, also recalls the aristocratic past.

At night I strolled the giant plaza in the city's center or spent evenings in the hotel. The hard currency bar was empty, but the Soviets were busying entertaining themselves in other places, including the room above mine. Partying all night is a prerogative of Russians, who tend to rise late and work not too awfully hard even when they're not on vacation. (One shouldn't take the generalization too far: there are many dedicated, hard-working people, but the absence of the Protestant work ethic, if that is indeed what has possessed us for all these years, does offer a marked contrast with American work habits.)

With the party raging above me, I gave up trying to sleep that night at 3 A.M. and didn't even think about complaining to the hotel management, as it would probably have done no good and I didn't particularly want to spoil their party. It may have been a birthday, or simply the last night of a vacation before they returned to the harsh realities of some provincial Soviet city. So, with a sigh, I got up, opened a warm bottle of beer I'd stashed on the balcony and ruminated in my diary as the sounds of a roomful of Soviets singing, dancing, and stomping their feet thundered through the uninsulated floor above.

"They are now absolutely howling like fools, butchering whatever song it is they're trying to sing, clearly as drunk as the devil on a moonlit night," I wrote in my notebook. "But at least they still know how to be human," I continued,

to interact with each other, sing songs, play guitar, clink toasts, sit around the table eating and drinking into the night. These are things we've forgotten how to do with our mass consumer culture, individual automobiles, fast-food drive-ins and general obsession with instant gratification. They live cramped together in small apartments, have bad movies and only just now videos. Most Soviets don't have individual telephones and going someplace requires taking crowded public transport. They can't jet around from city to city anytime they want, nor move to a new place to live, but as my friends above are reminding me, they *do* still know how to entertain themselves.

I caught up on sleep that afternoon and decided to attend the "erotic" evening show in the main dining hall that night. It featured singers, a juggling act, and finally (this was the erotic part) partially nude dancers singing "Yalta, *prekrasno*" ("Yalta, it's wonderful"), all of which took about an hour. "It's the exact same boring thing every night," the waiter told me, shaking his head.

When the dancers exited and the lights came up, I sat alone with my baked chicken, greasy fried potatoes, and wine. After a few minutes, music blared over the sound system and couples took to the waxed dance floor with great enthusiasm.

A young woman with light red hair sitting alone nearby asked me for a dance and afterwards we had our dessert and tea together. Lena, tall and shapely with a friendly smile that revealed a couple of gold teeth, was a schoolteacher on holiday from nearby Simferopol. She knew a little English.

As we chatted, another young woman whom I'd never seen before appeared and requested my presence on the dance floor. I complied, trying to remember if two young women in the same evening had ever asked me to dance in the United States. "Where are you from," the second woman, Genia, asked and when I replied "*Sayscha*" (USA), she cooed with delight. She was the daughter of a well-connected party official in Vladivostok, in the Soviet Far East, and was wintering in Yalta to escape the cold and twelve-foot-high snow drifts.

I returned to my original table, where I was joined by my first dance partner, Lena, who at that point had apparently decided to skip the preliminaries in view of the mounting competition. In perfect, deliberate English she said: "I want to have your baby tonight."

As I noted before, Russians tend to be direct. In a few minutes the show ended and I left the dining room, but not with Lena.

I departed the next morning for Kiev, the capital of Ukraine, which used to be the third largest Soviet republic when it still was a republic rather than one of the independent states of the Commonwealth. It was already evening when the Aeroflot jet landed and

I had to find my way to a cooperative—meaning quasi-private—rooming house somewhere in the city.

I came to terms with a taxi driver and arrived at the address I had been given by the university officials in Kazan, but despite my possession of a reservation that "absolutely guaranteed" me a room, the two young women lounging in the reception room with bored expressions on their faces told me there was no space. It was almost 11 P.M.

I was livid, of course, and railed at them in serviceable Russian, waving the "absolutely guaranteed" reservation under their noses. "This is not America," one of them shrugged, smiling cynically and pulling on her cigarette, "it's the Soviet Union." I told a Kazan friend about it later and he suggested they probably wanted a bribe. I never even thought of it.

Finally, one of the women said, "Wait a minute, isn't that new apartment prepared over on Such and Such Street?" The other woman looked doubtful but the first one insisted it was available, took my rubles, gave me a key, and advised me to take a taxi.

I got to the location and, after struggling with the door lock for three or four frustrating minutes, finally opened it.

I was sorry I did. Inside was a beaten-up couch with springs jutting out, no sheets, blankets, or pillows, no running water in the corroded bathroom or kitchen sink, and on the stove I interrupted a cluster of cockroaches dining on a pan full of month-old grease.

I was tired but not that tired.

I locked my things in the room, went out on the street, stamped my feet in the cold while people ahead of me in the queue finished their telephone conversations, and then couldn't get through to the clerks at the cooperative. It had been my intention to scream at them over the telephone. I returned to the room, struggled again with the lock, grabbed my things, and left. I caught my third taxi of the evening and directed the driver to the nearest Intourist Hotel. I managed to check in for rubles after an argument in which I lost my temper again because they insisted I pay the ruble price charged to foreigners, which was about six times higher than I had the right to pay by the terms of the clearly worded agreement I showed them.

I found these constant Soviet hassles enervating, but something would always happen soon after to make it all worthwhile.

In this case, I found God.

He was alive and well in Kiev. As I toured the city's famous cathedrals and a historic monastery the next day, I first became aware of the religious revival that was sweeping across the country, once the proud center of world atheism. As I would learn from subsequent travel and investigation, Kiev was not alone.

From Vladivostok to St. Petersburg, Soviets are returning to their renovated churches as *perestroika* and now the triumph of the "pro-democracy" movement have lifted restraints on religious expression. Before it was disbanded, even the Supreme Soviet passed a Freedom of Conscience law. The Russian Orthodox Church was locked in a legal battle to receive back property seized from it after the Bolshevik Revolution. Russian President Boris Yeltsin, who made it a point to appear with church leaders and to attend services on religious holidays even before he gained power, advocates complete freedom of religion.

While it is in many respects a typically sprawling and drab Soviet city, Kiev's cobbled streets and cathedrals capture some of the past of the ancient capital of "Kiev Rus." The place has known human habitation for 20,000 years, but has also been repeatedly sacked and plundered by invaders ranging from the Mongols to the Nazis.

After strolling the *Kreshchatik*, the city's main thoroughfare and a Soviet version of the Champs Elysées, I toured two of the most famous cathedrals, St. Andrew's and St. Sophia's, both now painstakingly refurbished architectural marvels—lots of gold, tile, religious paintings, icons, mosaics, and frescoes.

At both cathedrals, and most especially at the Monastery of the Caves, set high upon a craggy hillside overlooking the Dnieper, I got a real sense of the rebirth of religion.

Inside the sprawling compound of the monastery, founded in the eleventh century and known for its labyrinth of underground caves whose constant temperatures over the centuries have preserved everything from food to mummies, I witnessed an outpouring of religious sentiment. It was a bright, crisp Sunday and thousands of worshipers filed into the main cathedral to place thin brown candles on stands at the church altar, crossing themselves reverently and kissing Chrisitian icons held and wiped clean after every kiss by dark-robed priests.

Outside a sixtyish priest with a long grey beard, deeply lined brown skin, and charred yellow teeth spoke to a gathering crowd about the evil consequences of stifling Christianity in the USSR. "France, Italy, the USA, Australia—all love God!" he thundered. "It is only here that people have been denied God's grace—and look at the condition our country is in!"

Those standing in the circle around the priest nodded so vigorously in agreement that I expected to hear them say "Amen, brother" any moment.

At both cathedrals and the monastery I could almost sense the momentum of religious revival as well as see it all around me. The crowds were thick with people buying icons, placing money into the renovation boxes even as scaffolding and piles of wood and stone evidenced the ongoing reconstruction.

I commented on the size of the crowd to a middle-aged man who promptly explained that "Our people need something to believe in. They don't believe in the state, they believe in God, do you understand?"

I saw the same phenomenon played out in Kazan, St. Petersburg, Siberia, indeed every place I traveled in the USSR. Scores of Soviet acquaintances had religious icons in their homes and hundreds of women wore crosses on their necklaces. Everywhere churches were being reopened, refurbished, and patronized by growing crowds. I even saw American televangelists preaching on Soviet television and heard TV and radio advertisements for Bible study classes.

Many Soviets remained staunch atheists but even most of them favored religious toleration. One university colleague told me that she had recently obtained a Bible for the first time. "I am not a Chrisitian and I don't believe in the authenticity of the Bible," she explained, "but I was amazed as I read it to find that this was such a marvelous work of literature. I could not understand, I could not believe, that my country had forbidden us to have access to this great work."

Outside the Kiev monastery's ornate Trinity Gate Church, beggars and disabled people sat with small wooden bowls or cloth rags folded open to receive coins and rubles from passersby. One middle-aged woman squatted on a curb in front of her cup as her baby daughter, her dirty face raked with scratches from an apparent accident, slept fitfully in a carriage by her side. Harassed by the police before *perestroika*, beggars and the homeless now appear unimpeded in virtually all cities. Their presence and the religious

revival itself both attest to the economic collapse and the rever-
sion to ancient faiths now that the god of Soviet communism has
failed them. With the collapse of Marxism-Leninism, itself a quasi-
religion, came a revival of the prerevolutionary orthodoxy to fill the
spiritual vacuum of an increasingly desperate people.

Having taken in the main sites in Kiev on my first day in the city,
I decided the next morning to call the home of a couple whose name
I had received from an acquaintance in Yalta. The woman who answered, Larisa, promptly invited me to come to their apartment
that very evening. I arrived a little early and her husband was not
yet home, but Larisa ushered me into the kitchen for tea, where we
sat while her four-year-old daughter wheeled about the apartment
giggling and dancing for our amusement.

Larisa, a lithe and attractive 25-year-old Russian, blond-haired
with light blue eyes, had married Yuri, a Ukranian, after a week-
long courtship and moved to Kiev from her home in Siberia to live
with him.

On the kitchen shelves they had placed Christian icons, empty
cans and boxes of Western food products, and the obligatory red
and white Marlboro box. A framed one dollar bill hung on the wall
between the shelves.

After a half hour or so Yuri arrived home wearing a blue and
orange University of Florida Gators sweatshirt and carrying a plastic bag from which he took Camel cigarettes, a can of German beer,
and some presents for his wife and daughter. He had been to the
private market. We shook hands and Larisa opened a bottle of
champagne and set out some sausage, cheese, and bread.

As we spent the evening getting acquainted, they asked the usual
litany of questions about American life. Did I have my own car?
What kind was it? How much did it cost? How much money did I
make? Your houses are big, aren't they? It's only lazy people who
aren't well off in America, right?

As usual when I became acquainted with Soviets, they greatly
enjoyed having an American around and Yuri offered to take me on
a driving tour of the city the next day. I agreed.

Yuri showed up at my hotel with a friend of his, Oleg, both in
their mid to early 20s, and we caught a taxi and drove to the center
of the city. We passed by the Supreme Soviet of Ukraine, a handsome crescent stone building with high columns, upon which I com-

mented. "Yeah," said Oleg, "it was built before the communists, but they took all the best buildings for themselves."

On the street outside protesters marched waving the blue and yellow striped Ukrainian national flag, toting anti-Soviet signs alluding to the horrors of Stalin and Beria, his sadistic secret police chief, and calling for an independent Ukraine. Although none of us could have conceived of it at the time, by the end of 1991 Ukraine had achieved total independence under the framework of the new Commonwealth.

I asked Yuri and Oleg if most of their friends and acquaintances were anti-communist. "Yeah, it's all Lenin's fault," Yuri replied. "All he thought about was getting revenge for his brother, Sasha, and that brought on the October Revolution. We've been suffering for seventy years because of Lenin's brother," he snorted. According to Yuri's reading of Russian history, it was the tsarist regime's execution of Lenin's brother, who was implicated in the 1887 attempted assassination of Tsar Alexander III, that had brought on the Bolshevik Revolution.

I suggested that Lenin, while something of a fanatic (aren't all revolutionaries?), had a little more depth than they gave him credit for and that he couldn't be blamed for the subsequent Stalinist terror. The taxi driver, whom none of us had ever met before, had been taking all of this in and could no longer restrain himself. "What have the Communists given us?" he demanded, turning to look at me. "Seventy years of nothing. They promised everything and delivered nothing."

Well, perhaps the Gorbachev reforms could better the society, I offered meekly. "Yeah, maybe it'll get better over time but what good will it do me? I'm 55 years old and if things improve after ten or fifteen years I'll already be an old man. They've taken my whole life. My father also gave his whole life to them—he fought in the Revolution, Civil War, and Second World War, lived through Stalin and all the rest—seventy years of promises and nothing delivered!"

We were quiet for a moment and then all burst out laughing when the driver glanced at me through the rear-view mirror and said, "By the way, you're not connected with the KGB are you?"

That night I joined Yuri and Oleg at a restaurant where I met some of their friends. Like Yuri, Oleg, and the taxi driver, these people were anti-communist. I had, to this point, talked to a lot of different people in four Soviet cities, eighty percent of whom I estimated to be anti-communist.

I felt I was getting to know the Soviet people. And it was becoming clear to me that most of them detested Lenin fully as much as they loved God and the United States of America.

CHAPTER SIX

Winter of War and Reaction

AFTER ARRIVING IN Moscow and receiving a comfortable room in a cooperative apartment, I resolved to stick to the routine business of tourism. I spent my first full day visiting the Pushkin Fine Arts Museum and the Pushkin Literary Museum, which I thought would be a cultured change of pace from the racism and vodka of my Volgograd and Kiev acquaintances.

Having paid my respects to Pushkin, the great nineteenth-century poet who founded the modern Russian language before his tragic death in a duel over an insult to his wife, it occurred to me that Lenin himself might need a little cheering up, in view of the beating he was taking from the children of the revolution. So I proceeded to Red Square, took a place in the relatively short line, and shuffled through the dank marble mausoleum where he lies in state.

The story that one of Lenin's ears once fell off while a tour group filed through the mausoleum is no doubt apocryphal, but Vladimir Ilyich was not looking too well. His black suit and shiny black shoes were fine, but his body has flattened like a Russian *blini* (pancake) and his face would be sent back to the sculptor for reworking before he could gain a place in one of the world's finer wax museums.

The truth is that Lenin himself never requested and would not have approved of this Stalin-inspired and thoroughly ghoulish display of his remains having gone on for almost seventy years. There has been talk of removing him from his sacred perch and there is a precedent: in 1961 Khrushchev ordered Stalin's body removed after his eight-year stint alongside Lenin. Lenin's body should be removed and buried at his birthplace or perhaps he could occupy a stone monument together with Stalin, Brezhnev, Andropov, the American journalist John Reed, and other heroes of the Soviet past who lie buried inside the the Kremlin Wall behind the mausoleum. (Khrushchev, incidentally, was so despised that Brezhnev denied him a proper Kremlin burial and his body now lies in a cemetery adjacent to a Moscow convent.)

Lenin's tomb, like the Lenin museums and Lenin murals and memorials that existed in every Soviet city, served to perpetuate the myth of the infallible leader in a failed effort to maintain support for the communist regime. In any society the ruling elite promotes its myths and heroes to build popular support (like Lenin, George Washington was long deified in early US history), but the Soviets made a fetish of it.

Lenin murals, monuments, books, statuettes, and museums formed a major industry in the USSR until recent years. In Kazan, Party officials angered many locals in the late 1980s by building an opulent new Lenin Museum, with spacious carpeted halls and audiovisual displays translated into five languages, near the central Lenin monument at Freedom Square. Were the tens of thousands of Kazan residents who lived without indoor plumbing or telephones really supposed to appreciate this allocation of state resources? Such skewed priorities go a long way toward explaining the collapse of Soviet communism.

I had already been to the Lenin Museum in Kazan, but had yet to see the main one, a massive (red, of course) structure at the mouth of Red Square. Like the one in Kazan, the Lenin Museum in Moscow was virtually empty. Here was room after room, down long polished marble corridors on three floors, immaculately maintained and devoted to the hero of Great October—and no one cared. One can see a precise replica of Lenin's office, the greatcoat he wore when a would-be assassin's bullets ripped into his side, original copies of his theoretical works, but only schoolchildren (who have no choice after all) and a smattering of other visitors were to be found. Only five people sat in a thousand-seat auditorium when I viewed a scratchy old film on Lenin's life.

I think it was that chilly January evening, as I wandered through the streets of central Moscow, that the profound transformation underway in Soviet society really came home to me. I was still pondering Lenin's fall from grace when I arrived at Pushkin Square and saw gleaming over the right shoulder of the Pushkin statue the golden arches of the famed Moscow McDonald's. Across the square was Pizza Hut, with its long outdoor queue for rubles-paying customers, and its comfortable indoor booths for those few, mainly foreigners, with hard currency. A huge red and white electronic Coca-Cola billboard sparkled high above the entire square. Outside the McDonald's stood an almost human-sized Marlboro box next to an arrangement of smiling plastic Disney characters.

My stomach gurgled in anticipation as I strode purposefully across the square, through the underground tunnel below what used to be Gorky Street and up to the familiar glass doors of McDonald's, visions of Big Macs and salty American fries racing through my mind. As I attempted to go through the door, however, a Soviet policeman stopped me and said the Russian equivalent of "what do you want?," literally "I'm listening to you" (*slushaiu vas*). Already irritated by the Soviet penchant for limiting free access to places—and certainly never having been barred from a McDonald's—I responded testily, "I want to eat, whaddaya think."

"This is the exit," he said, pointing. "*There* is the entrance." I looked around the corner to where he pointed and saw on this cold Saturday evening the longest line I have ever seen in the Soviet Union or anywhere else. It stretched through streets, around buildings, up and down hills, to Vladivostok for all I knew for I could not see the end—literally hundreds of Soviets calmly waiting for their taste of an American *gamburger*, fries, and Coke, this even though all of the prices had recently been doubled for the second time in a year.

"Holy shit," I said, and the cop, needing no translation, laughed. I walked away, purchased a greasy meat pie and dripping ice cream cone on the street, and resumed my life as a Soviet. I reflected, however, that the emptiness of the Lenin Museum and the teeming, patient crowd paying homage at the temple of American consumerism spoke volumes about the transformation in Soviet society.

The next day, at 11 A.M. on January 17 to be precise, I called the US Embassy from a street telephone to inquire about a new shipment of books I was expecting for my courses in the second semester at Kazan State University.

"Oh, Professor Hixson," the aide in the Cultural section said, "you're on our list. I was just trying to call you. But since you're in Moscow, the Ambassador will be giving a briefing on the situation here in the main hall at noon and you are invited to attend if you'd like."

"A briefing on what situation?" I replied, thoroughly puzzled.

"Oh, you haven't heard?" she asked. "The war started last night and Iraqi students in Moscow have made threats against all Americans in the Soviet Union. We have reason to think those threats are credible."

The outbreak of the Gulf War was, of course, major news to a diplomatic historian, though hardly unexpected since I had been following events over my shortwave radio. I caught a taxi and headed straight for Chaikovsky Street, occasionally glancing over my shoulder to ensure that knife-wielding Iraqi students weren't on to me yet.

By the time I arrived, Soviet police had the Embassy surrounded and I had to show my passport to three people before I got in. The main auditorium was packed and people streamed out the doors as Ambassador Jack Matlock told us what a profoundly evil man was Mr. Saddam Hussein, who now had to be taught a lesson by the guardians of the free world. "I am proud that we are stopping him now," declared the bespectacled, balding diplomat, who wore a striped suit.

The roomful of diplomats, clerks, and functionaries buzzed with excitement, but also a sense of foreboding, as no one anticipated the easy victory the United States would win by pummeling Baghdad with smart bombs (not to mention the stupid ones that killed tens of thousands of innocent civilians). "Please don't spread rumors," the Ambassador intoned, "we're going to tell you everything we know, within reason."

Matlock concluded with his best attempt at a Churchillian exhortation to victory, leaving the stage to a troubled round of applause before an Embassy security official took over. "Every American institution in this city is under some degree of threat," he said, alluding to the unspecified threats by Iraqi students. "All mail will be screened, stamped, and X-rayed. If it is not stamped, don't open it. You must look in your vehicle and examine it when you leave it unoccupied. Don't get cavalier about it, you could jeopardize the whole embassy."

Clearly memories of the "Beirut massacre" of US Marines in the 1983 van incident were on their minds. Outside, breaking all records for Soviet efficiency, Moscow police cleared out the ever-present line of Soviet citizens waiting for exit visas while construction crews blockaded the entrance to the Embassy with huge concrete pylons designed to prevent a terrorist assault.

I spent the next two almost surreal days hovering around the television in a lounge in the new Embassy compound, watching CNN and feeling overwhelmed by my presence in this sparkling clean and plentiful oasis in the midst of the *defitsit* of Soviet society. The Embassy cafeteria served American-style food; there was an efficient post office to send mail west through Helsinki; the commissary shelves were stocked with groceries, soft drinks, beer, wine, and hard alcohol; *USA Today, Time,* and *Newsweek* abounded. It was a land of clean and mopped floors, sanitized toilets, gleaming white trash bins, and polished mahogany tables. It was, in short, like nothing I'd seen in the three and one-half months I had been living as a Soviet.

Returning to my cooperative apartment that first night in Moscow, I found that I could not take a shower because the water had gone off in the apartment building. Thus, when I returned to the Embassy the second day, I was surely the only American who carried around a plastic bag and wore the same clothes and unwashed hair as the day before. These were perfectly acceptable Soviet habits, but I stood out from the crowds that gathered in front of the television.

Stunned and quiet the first day, the Americans in the Embassy on Day Two became jubilant as news of the war came across CNN. They shouted "Yeah!" and cheered when the military censors graciously released the stunning film of the Iraqi Air Force headquarters and other buildings being vaporized by smart bombs. When CNN flashed to war protesters in San Francisco and Minneapolis, the residents of this outpost of democracy in the heart of the communist world booed, hissed, and suggested that the demonstrators "go live with Saddam Hussein if they love him so much!"

I felt very much alone in this crowd, as I looked around at the

sea of white puffy faces, freshly shampooed hair, bright new clothing, potato chips, and Snickers bars being washed down with
Coke while the United States pummeled an ancient third world
capital. I felt the revulsion that many third world residents must
feel at the spectacle of these wealthy, television-numbed Americans
cheering the slaughter that even discriminate aerial bombardment
was bound to effect. It was as if my fellow Americans were rooting
for their favorite sports team, or killing the space invaders in a computer game, taking an almost impersonal pleasure in the horror of
high-tech warfare against a helpless people.

Quite apart from my personal feelings about the war, which are
complicated, it was hard to maintain much respect for the Moscow
Embassy and its operations. Ever since a 1986 scandal when Marine guards traded petty state secrets for sex with KGB prostitutes,
the Embassy has restricted contact between its personnel and Soviet
citizens, thus limiting what our diplomatic people could learn about
what was actually happening in Soviet society. *Newsweek*, quoting
some of the diplomats themselves, called attention to this in a
May 13, 1991, article, appropriately entitled "Out of Touch in
Moscow."

At a time of revolutionary change in Soviet society, the US Embassy was indeed out of touch. I met scores of Americans in the
business and scholarly communities, most of whom knew a lot
more about the realities of Soviet life than the Embassy personnel, cloistered as they were in their English-speaking red brick
compound.

The Embassy did nothing to earn the respect of visiting scholars
and business people. "In other missions when an exchange scholar
arrives, he's met at the airport and treated like a human being," the
sympathetic Cultural Affairs officer, Ty Kemp, once explained to
me, "but not here. We just don't have the staff."

The Embassy not only offered no help with things like hauling
heavy crates of books needed for classes, but in fact sometimes harassed members of the scholarly and business communities in Moscow. The first time I went there, a US Marine sergeant, holstered
automatic pistol on his hip, did his Sergeant Rock imitation and
upbraided me for not knowing in which department an official I
needed to see worked. Full-color portraits of Bush, Baker, and
Quayle smiled down upon me as the Marine guard grilled me about

my business in the Embassy. "I'll never go down there again," said one historian friend, outraged over an unprovoked padding down search and verbal harassment he once received. "Why don't they just shut the whole fucking thing down—what a waste of money," an American businessman who had been traveling to the USSR for years told me. "Those people don't do shit."

While his emphatic judgment is too harsh, the Embassy was clearly in disarray, which is no doubt part of the reason Bush appointed Robert Strauss (who lasted just over a year) to replace Matlock in 1991. Not only was the Embassy failing to gather intelligence, but a fire that broke out on March 28 destroyed valuable communications facilities when Embassy officials let it burn for several minutes before admitting Soviet firefighters, whom they feared included among their ranks KGB spies. The Soviets contributed to the siege mentality of course with repeated espionage gambits, including building bugs into the walls of the new Embassy compound, which precipitated a protracted controversy and ultimately the decision to tear much of it down and start over again. Embassy officials only half jokingly called a church tower across the street "Our Lady of Perpetual Surveillance," since it had been known to house figures training binoculars on the Embassy compound.

Despite my contempt for a lot of what went on at the Embassy, I can't deny that I succumbed to the allure of Western material abundance that it represented in the midst of the *defitsit*. After weeks of relatively hard times in Kazan and on the road, I delighted in taking my meals in the Embassy cafeteria. I stared in wonder at the well-stocked shelves of the commissary, much as my friends in Kazan, whom I thought about at the time, might have done. To my amazement, however, Embassy officials forbade me to shop in the commissary, which serves annual dues-paying members only, but after pleading my case and describing conditions in Kazan, they grudgingly gave me a one-day pass to buy a sack of groceries.

After spending two days on Chaikovsky Street, I was ready to resume my life in provincial Kazan. The Iraqi students in Moscow proved as impotent as Saddam Hussein, mounting only a pitiful protest in front of the Embassy. No American, so far as I know, endured an attack from the Iraqis in Moscow. Nevertheless, when I stepped out of the Embassy compound for the last time and into the Moscow night, I really did find myself glancing over my shoulder in anticipation of Iraqi terrorists, who turned out to be only apparitions.

In addition to the carnage in the Middle East, a definite rightward thrust of *perestroika* made the winter of 1991 highly unsettling.

What Gorbachev, *glasnost*, and *perestroika* had been all about was an effort to reform Soviet socialism. However, by the end of 1989, with the disintegration of communist regimes across Eastern Europe, it became clear that the communist system itself was under siege in the USSR. Recognizing that he was losing control of the reform process, which now threatened to bring not only the end of communism but outright dissolution of the USSR, Gorbachev flirted with the reactionaries who later tried to overthrow him. The Soviet president rejected the "500-Day plan" for radical economic reform, placed sharp new restraints on *glasnost*, and veered toward authoritarian communism.

As the Soviet leader took on more and more of the trappings of a traditional party boss, Foreign Minister Eduard Shevardnadze stunned East and West by announcing in December 1990 his resignation as a "personal contribution, my protest against the advance of dictatorship." In mid-January, Soviet paramilitary forces seemed to confirm his suspicions when they unleashed brutal attacks in Riga and Vilnius ("Bloody Sunday"), the capitals of the independence-minded Baltic republics of Latvia and Lithuania, killing some twenty people.

At that point Boris Yeltsin broke off dialogue with Gorbachev, whom he, too, now accused of "bringing the country to the edge of dictatorship." Yeltsin declared that he had been mistaken to have ever placed his trust in Gorbachev and called for his "immediate resignation. . . . I have made my choice. I won't leave this road," declared Yeltsin, expressing his faith "in the support of the people of Russia."

On January 23 I walked but did not chant as tens of thousands of pro-democracy Muscovites marched on Red Square, shouting "Gorbachev resign, Gorbachev resign" even as the Communist Party General Secretary ordered the Army to make its presence felt in Soviet cities. This last action was taken ostensibly to combat a new "crime wave," but clearly the main purpose was to have a chilling effect on dissent. (Some soldiers eventually showed up on the streets in Kazan, but the rag-tag outfits never made much of an impact on the community.)

While all of this was going on, the United States, though pre-occupied with its splendid little war in the Persian Gulf, delivered a sharp official protest over the train of events, which threatened to undermine the new era of post-cold war cooperation, and President Bush backed away from plans for a February 13 summit in Moscow.

It appeared to me, listening to the Soviet news on *Vremia* as well as the Voice of America and BBC over my shortwave radio, that all hell was breaking loose. It was clear that *glasnost* had suffered crippling blows and that the violence in the Baltics and in other peripheral regions such as the Caucasus might soon infect the center and plunge the country into civil war.

Back in Kazan, however, although my friends paid some attention to these events, they were much more indifferent than I would have expected. They seemed preoccupied with their own day-to-day problems and reflected a certain resignation at having no control and no voice in the events taking place in their country. I concluded that the residents of Moscow, Kiev, and St. Petersburg were more heavily invested in *glasnost* and the pro-democracy movement than provincial Soviets, who were no less aware of what was going on but, far from the traditional centers of power, simply more accustomed to their inability to influence events.

Nevertheless, I did witness the shock on the faces of some of my friends in Kazan one Friday evening as we gathered for a typical session of dinner, drinking, and conversation. At 11 P.M. we turned on the television to watch the popular program, *Vzglad* (Viewpoint), one of the most probing and sharply critical new television programs of the *glasnost* era.

Vzglad featured two casually dressed, young commentators who regularly conducted interviews with outspoken officials and took up the most sensitive political and economic issues facing the USSR. As we got set to watch, the host who regularly introduced Soviet television programs appeared on the screen and said that *Vzglad* had been canceled "for political reasons" and would not be shown that night.

We were stunned. "Oh, this is not good, this is not good," observed Alec, one of my friends. "It means they are moving back to the old methods." "Well, that's our *perestroika*," said a young woman, Marina, as she snapped off the television, "no more freedom, no more *glasnost*."

Vzglad had been set to probe the reasons for Shevardnadze's resignation and Gorbachev's new director of national television, the censorious and now notorious Leonid Kravchenko, simply canceled the program as too sensitive. It never appeared again in Kazan during the course of my stay. (Yeltsin summarily fired Kravchenko after the failed August coup.)

During these weeks I also observed sharp changes in the newscasting on *Vremia* as a result of Kravchenko's decision that the people were tired of too much "negative" news reporting. When I had arrived in the country, *Vremia* reported the news about as straightforwardly as our own networks, which is to say that it followed the president around, reflected all sorts of prejudices, biases, and unproved assumptions, but stopped short of outright propaganda. In the wake of Gorbachev's rightward shift, however, *Vremia* began to air veteran party line broadcasters and to phase out or force into line the younger Western-style reporters who had seemed to represent *glasnost*.

The program launched highly partisan attacks on Yeltsin that coincided with Gorbachev's efforts to have him replaced as leader of the Russian Republic. *Vremia* devoted several minutes of praise to the patriotic "Army Day" celebrants in Moscow, but ignored the huge January 23 pro-democracy demonstration. The program even reverted to the most cliched reports of bumper grain harvests and happy farm workers.

In addition to appointing the reactionary Kravchenko, Gorbachev chose as his new Prime Minister the portly, crew-cut old-style communist Valentin Pavlov, who was destined for unpopularity and, in the wake of the failed coup, prison. I thought of my relatively well-off Volgograd and Kiev acquaintances, Andrei, Yuri, and Oleg, when Gorbachev issued an *ukaz* (decree) announcing Pavlov's first major "reform," one that required all fifty and one-hundred ruble notes to be turned in and taken out of circulation. This action apparently targeted just such people, those involved in black market activities who had accumulated a lot of rubles and whose alleged hoarding of them was now said to be holding back the Soviet economy and promoting inflation because too much money was chasing too few goods. The ruble conversion program allowed citizens to receive smaller bills in exchange for their large bank notes, but only if they could explain how they legitimately came to own them.

The program, which gave citizens three days to change their money, set off a virtual panic throughout Soviet society, including Kazan. All normal activity stopped and huge lines formed at banks and cashier's offices, some of which simply had to shut down to control the crowds.

As usual, it seemed as if the Soviets had found the most inefficient means of conducting the program. At the university, for example, everyone left their desks at once and took a place in mammoth queues at the cashier's office. They had to stand in one long line to turn in their money and receive a piece of paper authorizing them to receive the smaller bills in return, which they could do only after wading through yet another line. Angry people stood for hours on their feet, shaking their heads, and muttering "*uzhas*" and "*koshmar*"—"the horror, a nightmare"—especially when they had waited for hours only to find that the cashier had run out of money at the second window.

No one believed the currency reform would accomplish its stated purpose, especially with respect to organized crime. "The Mafia has long known that this was coming," one university official told me in a familiar refrain. "They changed their money a long time ago."

Almost everyone with whom I spoke resented what they perceived as the state's latest intrusion into their lives. "Everything Gorbachev does is against the people," one young Tatar woman told me, reflecting a widespread view in Kazan. "What a horrible man, I can't say how much I hate him."

"Gorbachev has got all of *his* money in a Swiss bank account," charged another angry citizen. "Every day there's a new *ukaz* and all they accomplish is to make our lives more difficult."

I myself had two 50-ruble notes and went with Galina Dmitrievna, of the university International office, to take a place in the massive queue in the university's main building. We used the presence of an acquaintaince to cut into the front part of the line, which is an accepted Soviet practice (the prevailing ethos is, if you know someone, take advantage of it.)

"Well, you see what kind of country we have," our friend in the line, Farrida, observed. "I've been here all morning and the line is barely moving. I'm sure Gorbachev is standing in line today," she snorted sarcastically. "It's very hard on the elderly people," she continued, "many of them will die. Their hearts can't take it—they're very upset and worried about their life's savings and to have to go stand in line all day—*uzhas, uzhas!*"

After she left and I waited an hour or so, Galina reappeared and announced that she'd used *blat* to arrange for me to get my money changed the next day *bez ocheredy*—without standing in line. I took a crowded bus home convinced that Soviet society was falling completely apart.

As part of his quest to keep that from happening, Gorbachev promoted the March 17 "all-union" referendum, which asked the electorate to vote yes or no on whether they wanted the USSR to remain a union of fifteen republics. Many people, in both East and West, considered the referendum a farce since it would be boycotted by some of the Baltic and Caucasian republics that had already decided that they wanted out. Moreover, the public had been given no voice in drafting the referendum statement, which left much unsaid about what the precise relationship between the center and the periphery would be.

Nevertheless, the referendum took place and was overwhelmingly approved in the republics where it was not boycotted. Once again, in Kazan I observed much public indifference concerning the referendum, yet there was also a surprising degree of support for it.

One cold February evening I discussed the referendum question over tea with a couple, a university professor and his wife, who supported Gorbachev's referendum. "Those who vote 'No' simply want to bring this government down," declared Nikolai. "They forget how much worse things could become. If you vote 'no' you are advocating nothing but disintegration."

At a dinner party one afternoon, I sat with five friends over chicken, beef stew, fresh bread, and lots of homemade wine as we discussed the impending vote. "I'm against it," said one woman, a factory administrator. "This kind of union we don't need to preserve." Her husband agreed, adding brashly that he wouldn't mind if the disintegration catapulted the country into civil war. "We need one," he said.

The host couple disagreed, however, saying they would vote

"*za*" (for) to preserve order and stability. Their daughter, Marina, a 21-year-old student, broke ranks, however, and said she wouldn't bother to vote. "It's just a meaningless question. If there was a vote for a president, or something that really meant something, then I'd vote."

I complained to another friend, a young Tatar woman from a working-class family, that night after night *Vremia* interviewed only Soviets who favored the referendum, whereas I had many friends and acquaintances who opposed it or were at best indifferent. I told her that I found the obvious television propaganda campaign offensive, but she said that she would vote *za* and dismissed my criticisms as irrelevant. "I'm not for it because of what's said on *Vremia*," she snapped. "I make up my own mind and so do other people."

"I'm for it, too," piped up her younger brother, Nail. "When we were all together as a country we were strong." I began to realize that part of the reason for the strong support for the all-union referendum was the pride many Soviets still felt in their country as a great power. A close friend, a university science professor named Ildar, agreed, observing that the approval of the referendum "was a vote for the Soviet empire. Gorbachev played the patriotic card."

For a time the support for the referendum puzzled me, coming as it did in the midst of Gorbachev's swing to the right. Over time I realized that the new restraints on *glasnost*, press and television censorship, the crackdown in the Baltics, Pavlov's reforms—those events didn't bother many of my Kazan friends as much as they bothered me, or as much as they bothered people in Moscow and St. Petersburg, where protest was much more widespread.

Some of the university intellectuals I interacted with in Kazan seemed more worried about the uncertainties and anarchic tendencies of the pro-democracy movement than a revival of traditional authoritarianism. "It is best for you to try to understand Russia as a country that is still in the Middle Ages," Ildar told me one evening. "We are not ready for democracy. A new culture cannot be built in a day."

To Ildar, who was far from a traditional communist, and to several other provincial Soviets, order and stability were more important than some idealistic vision of pure democracy, which he was convinced would bring on violent disorder. "Yes, it is bound to come," said Ildar. "Within five years the country will be in great turmoil. We may come out of it by, oh, about 2010."

The overwhelming support of the voters for the March 17 all-union referendum reflected some continuing backing for the existence of the USSR as a great power as well as fear of disorder that disunion represented in people's minds. Yet a high level of public indifference, confusion, and the boycott on the part of several republics rendered the referendum meaningless.

At the time I was still struggling to come to grips with Gorbachev. Did his turn to the right reflect his desire to return to traditional authoritarian methods, or was he doing the least that he had to do to placate the Party hardliners who later tried to overthrow him? We may never know for sure, but it is clear that when a potential crisis arose in March 1991, Gorbachev refused to take the action that would have led to bloodshed.

Just over a week after the referendum, a massive protest in Moscow culminated events that winter and pointed to the eventual defeat of Gorbachev's effort to reassert central party authority. Several hundred thousand Muscovites defied a ban on rallies, issued by Gorbachev and backed by fifty thousand troops, to march in the cold on March 28 in support of Yeltsin, whom Gorbachev was trying to have impeached from the Russian parliament for his declaration of "war" against the regime and call for Gorbachev's resignation.

There was a real possibility of massive violence in the capital until Gorbachev backed down, called off the ban on rallies, and allowed the demonstration to proceed unimpeded. From that point on, Gorbachev began to distance himself from traditional party-centered authoritarianism and toward a new rapprochement with Yelstin and the pro-democracy movement.

"The Gorbachev merry-go-round continues," I wrote in my diary in early May. "He's moving back to the left and he and Yeltsin have kissed and made up again. He's either totally indecisive or a genius of balancing opposing forces and keeping the country together. I'm leaning toward the latter today but who knows where Gorby, or Yeltsin for that matter, will be next week."

In retrospect it is now clear that the events I witnessed that winter were a dress rehearsal for the climax in August when the tanks stopped at the barricades outside the Russian Parliament building.

Upon his return from captivity in the Crimea, Gorbachev gave a spirited defense of the ideals of socialism, but within three days had no choice but to resign as General Secretary of the disintegrating Communist Party.

My friend Ildar, no partisan of Gorbachev, once observed that "no matter what happens, history must consider him a great man."

"Oh, please," responded his sister, "I must leave the room if you are going to speak like that about this awful man."

Their divergent views reflect the mixed emotions prompted by Gorbachev, the man who first allowed revolutionary change to unfold; then tried to rein it in; and ultimately saw his power, and his state, slip away.

But no matter how unpopular Gorbachev was and always will be with a broad segment of Soviet society, my friend Ildar had, of course, been right: Mikhail Sergeiyevich Gorbachev is a historical figure of towering proportions.

CHAPTER SEVEN

Godfathers and *Gopniki*

ஃ

I T W A S L A T E, around midnight, on a Saturday in early November. I had been inside all day, reading and recovering from some intense socializing the previous evening. I decided to go for a walk.

On the dark Kazan streets I saw the usual late-night sights: small groups of people standing on the corners trying to flag down taxis; wives or girlfriends struggling to prop up drunken male companions; stray dogs on maneuvers, their muzzles close to the ground sniffing for food.

After strolling for an hour or so, I rounded the corner of my apartment building and made for the door when suddenly a sixth sense compelled me to look up. On a three-foot wide concrete ledge above the entrance crouched a teenage boy, whose only logical purpose for being there was to leap down onto an unsuspecting victim.

The word *gopnik* comes from the root "gop," which means jump, apparently as in to "jump" someone. A *gopnik* was thus a kind of hood or street criminal.

I had just encountered my first one.

I continued walking toward the entrance but kept my eyes keyed on the shadowy figure on the ledge. He turned his face away and I walked quickly into the building. By the time I ran up the stairs and looked out the window, he was gone.

Fortunately for me, *gopniki* usually target women, who are more likely to be wearing valuable jewelry and may be easier to subdue. I spoke with a number of Kazan women who told me they no longer wore jewelry in public because they feared attack. Neighbors in my apartment complex spoke of an incident in which a *gopnik* had attacked a woman in the courtyard of our building at midday and had tried to rip off her gold necklace. Her resistance and the screams of a neighbor prompted him to abort the robbery attempt and streak away.

I had heard a great deal about crime and especially about Kazan's criminal youth gangs, a violent subculture so notorious that the "Kazan phenomenon" was known throughout the USSR. The combination of the violent street gangs and the Tatar "Mafia" had led to the city being dubbed "Little Chicago."

Having learned about the criminal activity before I arrived in Kazan, I experienced some trepidation about even going there, much less staying for ten months. Since the few Soviets I had spoken with in the United States seemed to know nothing about Kazan *except* for its violent reputation, I thought I might be in for some danger.

When I first arrived in Moscow, an American affiliated with the US Embassy seemed amazed at my destination. "Kazan!" he said incredulously. "That's a rough place. I had a friend who was almost beaten up there just for taking pictures of a group of guys on the street." Months later, after I had delivered a lecture at a prestigious institute in Moscow, one of the Soviet academicians took me aside and said: "Be very careful when you go back to Kazan. It is a very dangerous city."

The "Kazan phenomenon" first emerged in the 1970s when teenage boys, who had divided into neighborhood gangs based on individual housing districts, began to engage each other in violent turf wars. They would encroach on each other's neighborhoods to fight with chains, iron bars, knives, and even guns when they could find them. By the time the 70s violence peaked in 1979, the city had been terrorized and the most notorious gang leader, Zhavdat Khantimirov, had been executed for banditry before a firing squad.

The violence abated for a few years before flaring again in 1988–89, which meant that it was still fresh in people's minds by the time of my arrival. The popular national newspaper *Komsomolskaia Pravda* reported that every fifth boy aged 12 to 18 was a member of the 60 or so gangs in the city. Fourteen had been killed from 1985–89.

Gangs still existed by the time I arrived, but there was apparently only limited fighting between them. I spoke with many people who had witnessed incidents and I even met a few gang members, though none of them would talk to me. Gang members are sworn to strict codes of silence. The penalty for violating them can be death.

A little pile of stones and flowers, a crude memorial at the top of some steps in the center of Kazan State University, attested to the brutal retribution meted out by the gangs. The unofficial memorial marked the spot where a young gang member, an only child, had been stabbed and beaten to death while his girlfriend was held back screaming to witness the killing. The gang member had reportedly divulged information about his group's activities.

Once, while visiting with my neighbors in my new apartment in the Gorky district, which had been a center of gang activity, one of the young women in the apartment complex pointed to a teenage youngster walking by and whispered in my ear, "There's Sasha, he's a *nastoiaschii gopnik*," a real gang member. I later met Sasha and tried to broach the subject of gang activities, but he had nothing to say.

I gathered from my conversations with Kazan residents that the young hooligans (it's the same word in Russian as in English) were bored and disillusioned. Provincial life offered limited social options. The vast majority of youth had nothing but contempt for the *Komsomol*, the Communist Youth League, which had virtually required membership and participation in activities of all Soviet youth to age 29 before the organization collapsed under *perestroika*. The few options open to young people—television, the cinema, browsing empty store shelves, an occasional concert or sporting event—left them uninspired.

In the late 1980s, a highly popular documentary film asked the question in its title, "Is It Easy To Be Young?" Everyone agreed that the answer was "no."

"Our young people don't have anything to believe in," one middle-aged woman told me. "They don't have any faith in the future. This is why they become *gruppirovki* (group, or gang, members)."

The same problems confronted youth all over the USSR, but for some reason the gang violence had become particularly virulent in

Kazan—hence the "Kazan phenomenon." Others suggested, however, that Kazan really wasn't so unique: it was just that under *glasnost*, with the fiercely independent city newspaper, the *Evening
Kazan* leading the way, a great deal of publicity had been devoted
to the gang violence in Kazan, overshadowing what took place in
other cities as well. "It's all over the Soviet Union," several people
told me, "not just here in Kazan."

As I learned more about the *gopniki*, the fears I had brought
with me to Kazan faded. I learned to identify the young gang members by their appearance: they invariably wore aviator jackets,
sweat pants, and cheap Soviet tennis shoes. They smoked cigarettes
and chewed sunflower seeds, spitting the empty hulls out of their
mouths in public, even on city buses, like miniature woodchippers.

In general, young Soviet men, whether they were gang members
or not, embraced an unimaginative macho popular culture. Bruce
Lee, Rambo, and Arnold Schwarzenegger were their idols, reflecting
the widespread fascination with weight-lifting, martial arts, and
any movie that featured judo, kung-fu, or hairy-chested grenade-
throwing heroes. Even the North Korean movies, which are extremely campy propaganda, were popular with teenage boys and
young men.

After a while Kazan's male youth appeared to me as caricatures
and not very menacing. Moreover, by that time I understood that
they usually reserved their violent acts for each other. "I don't
worry about them," declared one Tatar man, Saidash, who lived in
one of the outlying districts of the city where gang violence had
been acute and police supervision minimal. "I've walked right past
them a thousand times. They're not interested in harming adults.
They only concern themselves with other gangs."

"I've never felt particularly threatened by them," observed another man, "except once a couple of years ago. I was downtown
late one night and I saw a group of them a couple of blocks away
walking together with candles. It was really eerie. I got out of
there."

During the violent waves, parents had simply kept their teenage
children off the poorly lit streets in an effort to prevent them from
being caught up in gang violence. Friends told me there were still
some sections of the city where only people who lived there or were

approved of could walk comfortably. Others might be stopped, beaten, and told they were not allowed to pass through the neighborhood.

As always in Soviet society, whom one knew made all the difference. One young woman, a university instructor named Jana, told me that she was once walking through a section of the city when a group of teenage boys barred her passage and began making threatening and sexually suggestive comments to her. "I told them, 'If you bother me you will have trouble with [a prominent local criminal whom her family knew]. They backed away from me immediately. Otherwise, I don't know what they might have done."

Her acquaintance with the local criminal paid off on this occasion, but the flip side was that he expected favors and loyalty from Jana and her family in return. On one occasion, for example, he asked her to do some translating work for him, which required her to travel a long distance. She tried to decline, under pressure of her university obligations, but he insisted and "said that there would be trouble for me and my family if I did not help him."

The type of on-the-street harassment that Jana encountered from the teenage boys was not at all unusual in Kazan, especially for women. I knew one young Tatar woman, Zulfiia, who simply could not go home alone at night because she lived in a neighborhood heavily patrolled by gangs of teenage boys. In essence, she had little choice but to be in by dark every night. Even at earlier hours she would be harassed on the street by the *khuligani*. "I just try to say, 'Oh, come on now boys, I'm too old for you,' or some other type of joke like that, and walk on by,'" she told me.

Zulfiia was describing a pattern of response that I found typical among young women in Kazan, a kind of street-smart appeasement. "You have to be clever to deal with them," my friend Guselle, a beautiful 21-year-old, dark-haired Tatar woman, explained. "You can't panic or scream or confront them—that's when they might really hurt you."

Guselle recounted a chilling incident in which a drunken *gopnik*, whom she had met once before, pulled her off the street and into a lot, where he menaced her with a knife and fondled her, all accompanied by an unimaginative stream of sexually explicit commentary. She didn't panic and tried to smile and joke while keeping him at bay. She encouraged him to continue to drink out of his bottle of vodka. As he got increasingly drunk, she convinced him to let her have a look at the knife, which she examined, turning it over in her hands for several minutes. Finally, when his attention waned, she slipped the blade into her own pocket. A few moments later, when the youth got up and began to stumble around looking for his knife, she slipped off into the night.

I was friends with a British woman who arrived in Kazan in the late winter to teach English at an institute in the city. One evening she was walking alone on a Kazan street when two men came up behind her and linked arms with her on either side in a mock attempt to stroll with her. She jerked her arms away and screamed, which they found enormously amusing and walked on, laughing. "There were other people on the street so it wasn't terribly frightening," she said later, "but if there hadn't been I would have been terrified."

Crimes against foreigners are increasing dramatically as many Soviets seek to steal the things they otherwise cannot access, principally dollars and clothing. Foreigners who live in dormitories set aside solely for them in Moscow and Leningrad are particularly vulnerable. An academic colleague of mine lived in just such a dormitory in Moscow with his wife and teenage son. As the boy returned home one night about 10, three Soviet teenagers mugged him, stripping off his Nike tennis shoes and running away with them. He was unhurt, though badly shaken.

I met another American who had had his pocket picked by two men in Central Asia. They took his passport and all his money. The police gave him enough money to return to Moscow, but asked him to look at some mug shots before he left. "I couldn't identify the thieves because all of the faces in their book were bloody and puffy since they had beaten them all up," he recalled, laughing. "I told them that they ought to take their pictures *before* they beat them up to give us a better chance to identify them."

Although I did meet some foreigners who were crime victims, the overwhelming majority of visitors never experience such problems.

Petty street crimes like pickpocketing, and even the gang violence of the *gruppirovki*, are small-time stuff compared with the activities of the Soviet "Mafia." I was surprised when I first heard the word, but after so many references to it I began to think of it as a Russian term. The "Mafia" usually referred to black marketeers, extortionists, and the criminal underworld that existed in every Soviet city. But people also used "Mafia" to refer to the Communist Party leadership, the bosses and managers of any industry, bureaucracy, or local government. In other words, any group that wielded power and was perceived to be above the law could be described as "Mafia."

As Soviet authority disintegrated in the late 1980s, the power of the criminal Mafia expanded. Although the regime denied the existence of organized crime until 1988, since then top police officials and even Gorbachev and Yeltsin publicly acknowledged its presence as well as the widespread network of activities ranging from gambling and prostitution to money laundering and demanding protection money. Moscow, St. Petersburg, Kiev—and most other cities—have already been divided into territories controlled by Mafia bosses. Under *glasnost*, newspapers, magazines, news programs, and Soviet movies called attention to Mafia activities.

Bribing and buying off public officials was rampant in Soviet society, allowing the Mafia to conduct its business with minimal interference. All citizens understood that the way to get things done is through giving bribes. The USSR had deteriorated to the point that it was becoming almost impossible to get anything done through official channels—so corrupt and inefficient had the bureaucracy become—but it was still possible to achieve almost anything if one had the means to offer a good enough incentive *na levo*, on the left, or on the side.

Months later, after I had returned to the United States, I got a call from a Soviet friend who was staying temporarily in the northeast. He loved the United States, of course, and was trying to secure permission from the Immigration and Naturalization Service to extend his work permit, but was running into problems. "The only problem with your country," he mused, "is that there is no one I can bribe to take care of this situation."

I told him that most of our bribing was upscale, in Washington and on Wall Street.

In addition to bribes and black market activity, the Soviet Mafia practiced extortion, usually in the form of demanding protection money. *The Evening Kazan* reported in January 1991 that three flower-selling kiosks had been burned to the ground by the local Mafia. The proprietors had simply failed to keep up their monthly payments to the criminals who controlled their neighborhood.

In Moscow it was common knowledge that the hundreds of co-operative businesses and restaurants that were opened under *perestroika* had to pay monthly protection money to stay in business. If they refused, their premises would be stormed, trashed, and burned by the local Mafia. "The same thing goes on all over the country, everywhere," my friends told me.

Sometimes criminal groups fight with one another for control over certain cooperatives or for sections of a city. In Kazan, criminal groups clashed periodically, usually in the middle of the night. Virtually everyone in my apartment complex in the Gorky district bolted up in bed one night about 2 A.M. when gunshots were exchanged in some sort of underworld dispute just outside our courtyard. No bodies were found, but incidents like these prompted many people to advise me not to return home or be out on the street for any reason late at night.

In virtually every city the local Mafia controls individual restaurants, which they have established as their private lairs. The citizens of these cities know the restaurants and other places where the black marketeers operate. I was warned to stay away from a couple of restaurants in Kazan, which the local Mafia dominated.

I followed this advice because I didn't want local criminals to know that a dollar-carrying, Reebok-toting American was in their midst, but I did get to know some Mafia members in Kiev when I visted there in January. They were Yuri and Oleg, with whom I had become acquainted through a mutual friend whom I had met in Yalta. As they showed me around Kiev (see Chapter 5), it became clear that they were part of the growing breed who operated outside the system in return for high salaries and access to Western products.

I first became aware of their work when I stopped off with Yuri and Oleg at a beer-dispensing kiosk in Kiev. We went around back and inside the shed-like building where I was introduced to the tattooed proprietor and given a large *stakan* of beer while they talked business, smoked cigarettes, and dispensed the watered-down *pivo* (beer). During the course of the conversation, I caught enough to understand that all were involved in black market activities and were affiliated with an extra-legal organization in Kiev.

I questioned Yuri and Oleg about their activities when we went out to dinner later that night. Tongues had been loosened by several rounds of vodka and they spoke openly about their black market activities. It turned out that they worked for a "godfather"—their term—one of six that purportedly operated in Kiev.

Yuri and Oleg performed a number of routine tasks, ranging from driving to Moscow or St. Petersburg to pick up goods or deliver cash, to policing the proprietors of the beer-dispensing kiosks. All such proprietors had to pay protection money to stay in business. If they refused, the local Mafia—people like Yuri and Oleg—would simply burn down their kiosks.

Yuri had been a soccer player on the Ukrainian national team—a successful *sportsmahn*, as the Soviets refer to athletes. "Until three years ago I didn't drink or smoke," he added, tugging on a Marlboro and nursing a mild hangover.

"Do you miss playing sports?" I asked.

He shrugged as if the question was irrelevant: "It doesn't pay any money."

As a result of their affiliation with their well-known godfather, Yuri and Oleg garnered a 3,000-ruble-a-month salary—about 10 times the Soviet average in 1991—and gained other perks as well. For example, Yuri wore a slick black leather jacket and South Korean-made tennis shoes, typical Mafia garb that no ordinary Soviet worker could possibly afford. They also got access to goods that they sold on the side. "Walter, if you are interested in religious icons," he told me, "I can get you the very best and for a good price." I told him I had no use for religious icons and he didn't press me.

When we arrived at "their" restaurant, a fashionable riverfront establishment, we received a choice table by a window overlooking the Dnieper. The moment we arrived, the waiter came promptly to our table—an exceedingly rare occurrence in service-unconscious Soviet restaurants—and took our orders, prompting Yuri to comment "He's the best, we always get him."

"Oh, he's your friend then," I remarked idiotically.

"Nah," said Yuri, "he's not a friend: he works for a living and we don't," to which he and Oleg roared with laughter.

As we ate and drank they explained that they bought and sold the one-armed-bandit slot machines that appear in hotel lobbies (but take only tokens) all over the USSR. The local Mafia also set up card games in which they tried to involve wealthy citizens as well as amusing themselves. Yuri himself said he once lost thousands of rubles, which he hadn't found so amusing, and had since given up gambling. He added that one man had lost 100,000 rubles, and had paid up.

"What if he hadn't paid the debt," I asked, "would he have been beaten or killed?"

"He might've been beaten up," Yuri said, "but more important his reputation in Kiev would've been destroyed."

I asked if there was violence between the six Mafia "families" in Kiev. They were silent for a moment and then Oleg replied that "things are pretty calm now. There was a conflict a month ago, but they [Mafia leaders] all met and agreed that a war now would hurt everyone."

However, added Oleg in a whisper as he leaned across the table, before the Mafia leaders had settled their disputes he had witnessed an incident in which two men who were members of a rival gang had been punished for some transgression. The two men had both of their hands hacked off in Oleg's presence. Members of his own group performed the act.

"You mean they completely cut off both their hands—and you saw it?" I asked incredulously.

"Clean off," he replied, "and I saw it."

"Didn't you feel bad about it?" was all I managed to say in response.

"Hey, they were guys who wanted to cut off *my* hands!"

It occurred to me later that Oleg may have been telling tales for my benefit, but I don't think so. I believed him and was eager to hear more, but at that moment a group of seven Soviet men in their late teens and early twenties, wearing the characteristic leather jackets, came up to our table in the restaurant. I eyed them apprehensively, but Yuri said "Don't worry, they're ours" and laughed.

They pulled up chairs and the group began talking rapidly together before focusing on me. One asked if I wanted to change dollars for rubles, but Yuri cut him off and told them not to harass me. "*Ladno*" (okay), the youth said, "but take a look at this for me." He took out a faded five dollar bill, a Silver Certificate— issued at a time when our currency was backed by silver, rather than the current "good faith and credit" of the hopelessly indebted US government—and asked if it was valuable. He flashed a big grin when I told him that it was indeed worth more than $5, though I couldn't say how much more. "Hang on to it," I advised.

A couple of the young men shared a hand-rolled cigarette at the far side of the table and I suddenly realized that they were smoking marijuana. At the same time I noticed that it was getting late and the restaurant was virtually empty. I became slightly unnerved. "Uh, it looks like they're closing, shouldn't we be going, Yuri?" I asked.

"Nah, we can sit here all night if we want. This is *our* place."

A few minutes later I tensed as a Soviet police officer approached the table and told us it was indeed time to be moving on. "Aw, don't rush us," said Yuri, his chair tilted back and feet perched on the table. "We've got an American brother here. Hey, show him your passport, Walter."

I handed him my passport and the young cop flipped through it, nodding with approval. "A real American," he grinned, looking down to me at the table. "Okay," he said, and ambled off.

This, I reflected, was the Soviet police state I had heard so much about.

My friends in Kazan and elsewhere would just laugh when I raised the question of police protection against criminal activity. There was none. There were police, of course—the *militsiia*—but they are poorly paid, many are said to be corrupt, and they do not, to understate the matter, display a commanding presence on the streets.

We stayed another half hour at the restaurant and then left. Yuri and Oleg escorted me back to the hotel and tried to convince me to cancel my plane ticket and stay another day or two in Kiev. "We have connections," he explained. "We can get you a ticket anytime, anywhere in the *Soyuz*, never have to wait in line," but I told them no thanks, I had to see someone the next day in Moscow.

After spending time with Yuri and Oleg in Kiev, the Soviet Mafia, like the *gopniki*, appeared far less sinister than they had before. The Mafia operated more or less openly all over the country because Soviet power was no longer real enough to oppose them and because the "shadow economy" they operated helped move goods and services around, albeit at inflated prices. The country needed a mixed economy and the Mafia was trying to do its part.

Most Soviet citizens accepted the existence of the Mafia as a fact of life, but many were disturbed at the rise in crime and growing brazenness of criminal elements, all reflecting the general disintegration of their society.

"It's depressing," observed an American scholar, a Soviet specialist who had been coming to the country for years. "The people don't believe in anything now, there's no morality. They're into all sorts of illegal and unsavory things now. Before there was corruption, sure, but most people knew it was wrong and felt guilty about it. Now they don't care. You see, there was something to this communism stuff."

As long as people met only roadblocks and frustrations in their efforts to advance through legitimate means, however, the lure of criminal activity would attract more and more followers.

Many Soviets thought that I must be shocked or feel threatened, as some of them were, by the level of criminal activity in the country. I tried to explain to them that a high level of criminal activity, both violent and white collar, was hardly novel for a citizen of the United States.

As usual, my Soviet friends would have none of it. Very few of them would believe that our problems with crime might be as bad as theirs, much less worse.

They were determined to be the best at something.

CHAPTER EIGHT

Education in Decline

"What kind of car do you have?"

"What are your hobbies?"

"Have you ever met Arnold Schwarzenegger?"

"What are your impressions of our country?"

I was standing on the stage in a spacious auditorium at the Kazan special school for mathematics students, trying to field the wide range of questions shot at me by a group of twelve- and thirteen-year-old boys and girls, who had clearly overcome their initial shyness in front of the American.

"What do American kids do with their free time?"

"How big are your houses?"

"Where have you traveled?"

On and on the questions came, an endless stream for over an hour. As I looked out at the audience, I noticed that the children wore bright clothes of their own choosing now that the once mandatory blue school uniforms (*forma*), with red kerchiefs for girls, had been made optional. They were intelligent and respectful, though their teacher occasionally admonished them for sharing whispers and giggles during the course of our meeting.

I spoke to them in Russian, though when we hit an impasse a couple of the students chipped in with halting English. There were thirty-five students, roughly one-third Russians, one-third Tatars, and one-third from mixed marriages. They all seemed to get along well and, in response to my direct question on the subject, said that they had no nationality problems in the school.

The children spoke freely and honestly, as did their teacher, Natalia, whose son was one of the students. The kids said they liked the school, but groused good naturedly about the upcoming final examination. When I asked them what they thought about the political and economic crisis in their country, or if they thought about it at all, their youthful grins gave way to a concerned silence before one dark-haired Tatar girl said quietly, "We think about the bad situation in our country, but we don't know what will happen."

Afterwards they crowded onto the stage as their teacher presented me with a huge bouquet of flowers and some old Soviet coins and stamps.

These youngsters, like most of the bright kids that I met in scores of private homes all over the country, left me with a favorable impression of the Soviet primary and secondary school system. Overall, basic educational skills impressed me during the course of my ten months in the USSR.

In their zeal to attack everything having any relationship to the communist past, people forget that the Bolsheviks succeeded in converting a backward agrarian people into a literate mass society. Similarly, in their glee over the collapse of communism, many Americans forget that the Soviet educational system—with the exception of politically charged subjects like history, literature, and philosophy—probably worked better than our own, at least at the primary and secondary levels.

However, the economic and political crisis in the country is gutting the educational system today. Higher education particularly, which I had much more direct experience with in my role as a visiting lecturer at Kazan State University, appeared to me to be in the midst of collapse. Although I met very many intelligent and capable people at the university, as well as in Moscow and in other cities, there can be little doubt that the higher education system desperately needs reform.

Since 1930, the Soviets have made primary and secondary education obligatory to age sixteen, free of charge, and accessible to the entire population. Primary and secondary students are not segregated according to ability levels and all are subjected to a uniform curriculum that includes chemistry, physics, mathematics, and foreign languages, subjects that many American kids have the freedom—and the inclination—to avoid. Pupils also go to school on Saturday; otherwise, their vacation times are roughly similar to ours.

Schoolchildren can attend special schools, like the one I visited, where certain subjects are taught more intensely in anticipation of the students pursuing a career in that particular area. The kids I met would go on to study mathematics, or a related field, at the institute or university level. In the foreign language special schools, most subjects are taught in the foreign language itself. During the course of my stay I met several people who had attended English language special schools. Their English was superb.

My negative impressions of the Soviet higher education system in part reflected my involvement in the most problematic field of study in the USSR—history. When Gorbachev's *glasnost* led to the exposure of the realities of the Stalinist past, people realized they had been deceived by the Party and its historians. The old examinations and history books were thrown out, but new ones have yet to be written. And in a society where it was difficult to get fired from a job, even for incompetence, the old-school historians remained entrenched.

Though I gave scores of lectures, seminars, and private talks, both within and outside Kazan State University, I encountered so many frustrations that I sometimes felt, though the judgment was too harsh, that my Fulbright Lectureship was a failure.

My History Department colleagues proved to be a great disappointment. Almost all of them were perfectly friendly but they didn't really know what to make of me and we couldn't communicate in any depth about intellectual subjects, partly because of the language barrier, but also because of their timidity. The top specialist in US history, for example, avoided contact with me, even after I presented him with several books and made it clear that I'd like to exchange ideas. He was not really very interested in US history and feared exposing his limited knowledge of the subject, even though I tried hard to show no inclination to be judgmental.

Another departmental historian, an older man who I was told had a past affiliation with the KGB, came to my inaugural lecture and sat respectfully throughout. But when the question-and-answer period continued for more than twenty or thirty minutes, he suddenly roared: *"Khvatat!"* ("enough!") and the session broke up. On a later occasion, when I asked someone to repeat or clarify something they'd said in Russian, he interjected, "Don't pay any attention to that. He understands our language perfectly, he just acts like he doesn't. He's reporting everything to the FBI." (I never have figured out why he didn't select the more infamous CIA.)

Most of these comments were said with a laugh, but they carried an edge and I think he really believed what he said. "You've got to understand," one close friend told me later, "our people have been told all their lives that Westerners are spies, so they can't really help but to believe it."

It became clear to me early on that most of my history colleagues in Kazan, long established in the university, hadn't been infected with the spirit of "new thinking" and *glasnost*. They didn't bother to schedule any lectures for me until the first semester was more than half over, even though I indicated that I was eager to begin. Even then it took the intervention of a vice rector to locate an available classroom.

At the start of the second semester, one of the History Department higher-ups, whose job during the Brezhnev years had been to go from department to department in the university ensuring that professors inculcated Communist Party values in the classroom, scheduled my lectures at an inconvenient time and in a room that held only twenty people.

When I arrived the first day, only four students sat in the room. There had been no announcement of my presence on campus and no opportunity for students to schedule my course.

I confided to a close friend, a KSU professor, that I couldn't understand how I could come thousands of miles to teach in Kazan, only to have the university fail to schedule any courses for me. I told him I could only assume that there was some sort of effort underway to obstruct my work, but he replied, "I doubt that this is aimed at you personally. It's simply the condition of our country at this time. No one is thinking about anything, no one is doing their work, everyone is upset about the state of our society."

I finally got my second semester teaching schedule straightened out when the Vice Rector for Science, Andrei Nikolaevich Salamatin, with whom I had become friendly, intervened and arranged for me to teach in a large lecture hall. My friends in the International Office put up a large full-color poster advertising my lectures and they were subsequently well attended.

It was a small victory for *glasnost* in Kazan.

The environment was much more professional in Moscow, where my Fulbright colleague, Peter Walker of the University of North Carolina, was lecturing on the history of the American South. Peter, on his second tour at Moscow State University, largely at the initiative of his gregarious wife, Daryl, enjoyed his contact with the Soviet scholars, though he resented having his spacious university apartment bugged by the KGB, as he felt sure that it was. "We'd better be careful what we talk about, huh?," I observed one evening after arriving for a visit. "Ah, screw 'em," Peter roared, gesturing at the invisible ceiling microphones.

The Moscow State University historians expressed no interest in my offer to arrange a seminar on the cold war and only four students showed up for an informal chat in the History Department. And two of these were American exchange students! However, Peter's Soviet colleagues did graciously set up a lecture for me before a group of historians at the Soviet Academy of Sciences, which proved both stimulating and revealing.

I gave a talk on my main research field, the history of US foreign policy since World War II, arguing that the West had "won" the Cold War because of the appeal of its material success, consumer culture, and democratic idealism. In short, the allure of the West overwhelmed the unfulfilled promises of the Soviet Communist Party. However, I went on, the United States had needlessly over-invested throughout the cold war in a militarized approach to containing communism; had intervened in destructive peripheral wars such as Vietnam; and had compromised its democratic principles by supporting neo-fascist regimes across the globe. None of these things, I concluded, was ultimately responsible for winning over the Soviets and East Europeans to our way of thinking.

I delivered the talk in English, a language that posed no problems to this large group of Soviet scholars, who sat around polished oak tables in a comfortable seminar room. They also showed a sharp knowledge of Western literature on the cold war.

Although I received many sincere compliments on the lecture and they treated me very graciously, it was clear from their questions that many of these Soviet specialists thought I had been far too hard on the United States. They didn't address specific points I had made as much as object to my overall tone. In one instance

I was afraid that one of them might even charge me with the ultimate offense—being a communist—but he settled for labeling me a "radical revisionist."

The previous year a prominent American historian, Eric Foner, who had lectured in Moscow, encountered the same phenomenon when he discussed the failure of Reconstruction after the US Civil War. "Nothing I said would have seemed particularly controversial to American historians," Foner later wrote, "but my talk was not, shall we say, greeted with enthusiasm. Listeners praised my research but seemed puzzled by my 'oppositional' stance."

The viewpoints expressed by some of the members of the Academy of Science mirrored those of Soviet society as a whole. The prevailing view was that the United States was a model society whose conduct in the cold war could hardly be faulted. The USSR alone was guilty.

History is not the only subject to have been thrown into disarray as a result of *glasnost*. One close friend, a Tatar woman named Guselle, who taught philosophy at an institute in Kazan, recalled her "horror" five years earlier when the realities of Stalinism were revealed to her for the first time. Before receiving her position, she had studied philosophy at Kazan State University and written and defended her dissertation on Marxist-Leninist dialectics.

"At first, when I began teaching I took the straight position that these were the facts, this was the truth, and that was it. Then to be told that all I had learned was lies—*uzhas!* (the horror)."

At age thirty-one, Guselle was already a burned-out Soviet academic, one of many I encountered. "I don't know what to do," she continued. "I have new courses to prepare and all the existing literature is worthless, but the new works have not yet been published." Guselle's disillusionment left her with little energy for her work, which included a heavy course burden and a salary so low she was contemplating taking on a part-time job counseling juvenile delinquents at night.

Moreover, she had little credibility with the students at her institute as a result of the cynicism bred by the myriad revelations of past state-sponsored lies. "They don't believe anything now. They tell me I am a communist and that I'm trying to teach them lies," she laughed.

Many students I spoke with confirmed Guselle's observations.

"When I was in school," a recent university graduate related, "they told us that we had the best country in the world. In America everyone was without a home and without jobs. And we believed it. I thought, 'How lucky I am to live in the Soviet Union,'" she concluded with a bitter, ironic smile.

While I made most of my academic contacts through the History Department at Kazan, I also spent a lot of time in the Department of English, where my second-semester translator and very close friend, Leonia Nickolaevich Sidorov, had taught for several years. Leonia, an ethnic Russian who spoke almost perfect English, was a fifty-three-year-old specialist in English who had successfully defended a dissertation on American history. Leonia, however, couldn't abide the intellectual blinders that the State placed on historical interpretation.

After switching to English as a specialty, he received his first assignment to go to work in faraway Uzbekistan, which he suspected was punishment for his failure to join the *Komsomol*, the Communist Youth League, where membership used to be *de rigueur* for all Soviet youths between the ages of 14 and 29. (I met another man who recalled that his twenty-ninth was the happiest birthday of his life precisely because it meant that he could quit attending *Komsomol* meetings.) Leonia himself never joined *Komsomol* in part because his parents, both opera singers, kept the family on the road for most of his childhood, but also because he had no desire to take part.

In job placement interviews, however, Soviet officials virtually demanded membership in the *Komsomol* before dispensing a good work assignment to an applicant. "You would simply be considered to be defying convention if you did not join the *Komsomol*," Leonia explained. Young people who hadn't worn the badge of Lenin, donned red kerchiefs, or listened to countless speeches about the heroic path of Soviet socialism could not be fully trusted. Even before the victory of the pro-democracy movement in the summer of 1991, millions of youths, the vast majority of them, had dropped out of *Komsomol*.

After teaching in Uzbekistan for several years, Leonia made his way back to Kazan State University, where he gained employment in the English Department. Leonia's phenomenal mastery of

English—I managed to teach him one word, the always useful "oxymoron," in the course of five months of close friendship—stems from his early childhood exposure to the language.

As a very small boy his father brought home an American canned good sent over as part of US lend-lease aid during World War II. He found the contents of the can (we decided it was probably Spam) to be delicious. "While I ate this food I marveled at the colorful label and the strange writing in a different alphabet. Ever since that moment I have been obsessed with English."

He also vividly recalled an experience as a young boy when he obtained a frayed copy of the 1941 Christmas issue of *Life* magazine, which had come into his possession in Perm, a city in the Urals, by way of a Soviet serviceman who had gotten it in Japan of all places. "I recall looking again and again at all of the colorful pages and the advertisements in this magazine and I thought 'What a rich place this America must be.'"

As he nurtured his love of English as a teenager, Leonia spent several hours a day—"much to the chagrin of my parents"—listening to popular music programs via Western radio. A shortwave radio fanatic (he owns four of them), Leonia has since his youth listened to the BBC, Voice of America, Radio Liberty, and other foreign broadcasts. He still recalls the distinctive voice of deejay Willis Conover, who emceed the popular Voice of America program, "The Jazz Hour." Leonia remains a jazz fanatic and takes turns with a small group of friends hosting jazz parties, which are always held on the birthdays of prominent jazz artists like Ella Fitzgerald and Dizzie Gillespie.

Leonia once told me a remarkable story that illustrates the appeal of Western music and popular culture dating to the early postwar years. He explained that before tape recorders were available in the USSR, enthusiasts of Western music would perform what they called "recording on the bones"—making crude but servicable homemade recordings on discarded sheets of X-ray film. The *samizdat* recordings would then be passed along and traded among friends.

Leonia's facility for English not only attracted him to American popular culture, but also nurtured his doubts about official Soviet versions of news events and world politics. When able to listen in over periodic jamming, Leonia realized by the mid-1950s that the party censors sometimes distorted and more often ignored pertinent news and information.

As a result, by the time of the 1956 Soviet repression of Hungary, he had grown distrustful of the regime and expressed some of his criticisms so openly that his dissent came to the attention of Soviet security authorities. That may have been part of the reason why Leonia, despite his obvious facility for English, had no opportunity until *perestroika* times to travel to the West to sharpen his skills in the company of native speakers.

Finally, in the fall of 1990, and then largely as a result of his wife's persistent efforts on his behalf, Leonia received permission to spend a semester in Edinburgh, Scotland, living with a British family and studying English. He cherished the experience and longs to repeat it in the United States or some other English-speaking country.

As I got to know Leonia, I realized that he found himself in an ironic position as Soviet society disintegrated around him. Whereas in times past he had been considered a potential dissident—what with his love of English broadcasts, his strong opposition to Soviet intervention in Hungary, Czechoslovakia, and Afghanistan, and his penchant for striking up conversations with visiting foreigners— many now viewed him a reactionary because he refused to condemn socialism in its entirety. "Lots of people, many of them are the diehard communists of yesterday, have gone radical today," he explained. "You know it's very easy to jump on the bandwagon. I'm sort of proud of myself that I've more or less kept my principles. I still believe that socialism has something good about it and that we should try to preserve some of its features, that we should not throw out the baby with the bath water. But it takes only saying that today to be branded a reactionary or even a Stalinist."

Despite his hope that some of the positive features of socialism could be preserved, Leonia had been impressed by what he saw in Scotland, had difficulty readjusting to Soviet society upon his return, and longed for another opportunity to visit the West. He was far from alone in his desire to travel to the West. Understandably enough, virtually every English instructor I met at Kazan State sought the same opportunity and many of the younger instructors have yet to get their chances. As with the competition for scarce goods under the *defitsit*, the competition for scarce opportunities like traveling to the West often provoked bitterness and recriminations within the English Department, where decisions tended to be made on the basis of *blat* rather than through an orderly process.

At the invitation of Leonia and Simon "Doog" Cockell, a talented British linguist and visiting instructor of English, I gave a series of seminars for language teachers on contemporary American life. Everyone in the English Department was extremely receptive, as interest in the language, and especially "American English," was at an all-time high.

Many Soviet instructors taught intensive English courses, which met for three hours, five days a week, for several weeks. They played Western rock music, sang songs, and tried to make learning a foreign language enjoyable.

Enrollment in English courses was skyrocketing in the USSR as a result of increasing contacts with the West, the growth of market relations, and the desire of large numbers of people to leave the country altogether. I often visited these classes for tea and conversation and met a wide range of people, from academics who wanted to improve their skills in English, to Jewish emigrants trying to prepare for life in Israel or the United States.

I met people in other departments, like Kamil, a young graduate student in mathematics from a Tatar village, who studied English with hopes of enrolling at a Western university. Kamil, like many others, reflected the despair of young Soviet scholars who see limited opportunities in their own country and imagine that there are no such limitations or burdens in the West.

"It seems that nothing is more coveted by educated Soviets than to get out of their country for an extended, if not permanent, stay in the West," I wrote in my diary one day after returning from the university. Scores of them attested to the popularity of English as a means of access to the West when they poured into an auditorium on campus one day to hear two visiting Americans describe the opportunities that were available through scholarly exchanges between the United States and USSR. The costs of language and graduate school examinations were prohibitive for the vast majority of people in the room, but just being there and dreaming about the idea of going to the West gave many of them a vicarious thrill.

While as a native speaker I was often in demand in the English

Department, I gained relatively little exposure to scientific departments on campus, which perhaps skews my perspective since science does represent the strength of the university. Kazan State, the second oldest university in the country after Moscow State, is one of the most prestigious in the USSR, largely on the basis of its reputation in mathematics and science.

Even in these fields, however, there was widespread dissatisfaction with the low pay and constraints on scientific research. One physics professor friend, a Tatar in his mid-thirties named Ildar, complained that the central state bureaucracy for scientific research stifled creativity, individual advancement, and the progress of science generally.

His major charge was that state committees on science—which he referred to as the "scientific Mafia"—exercised excessive authority over individual research. "They decide what a scientist must work on," he complained. "You don't even have the opportunity to make your own choice or to follow your own curiosity and intuition. They say 'We don't need this, we already have this, we need you to work on *that*.' It is bad for the cause of science," he went on, gesticulating emotionally. "A scientist must be free to apply his curiosity and ingenuity to a topic that appeals to him."

According to Ildar, scientific researchers only get the freedom to pursue their own research interests when they have advanced through the system over many years. "But by this time very often they are older and no longer feel like doing any real scientific work," he observed. "Besides, they have spent most of their time learning how to manipulate the bureaucracy rather than devoting their energies to science."

Like the state bureaucrats in Moscow, powerful deans and department chairs at Kazan State University impeded constructive change. Departments were headed by well-connected traditionalists, some of whom had been department head for more than thirty years and were closed to innovation. Often their wives or husbands would run another department and their sons and daughters would gain employment through them, regardless of capabilities. Nepotism was rampant.

Teaching jobs often depended on *blat*, whom one knew, rather than merit. Farrida, a young Tatar woman whom I got to know, was highly skilled in her field but could not gain a regular appointment simply because she had no close personal connection with the department head, who had been in office more than thirty years and tended to dole out jobs to friends whom she could trust to remain loyal to her, in the manner of a political ward boss.

Farrida performed clerical work as well as carried a heavy teaching load, all for extremely low pay, even as she worked on her dissertation. Most people understood that the department head was incompetent and that the system victimized people like Farrida, who had better skills and qualifications than some of her superiors, but nothing was being done. "It's pretty depressing," she admitted, "but sometimes you just have to laugh when you think about the way things are done here."

In addition to the professional frustrations, Kazan State University, like most Soviet institutions, was often a grim place to work. The classrooms, located in two towers, the highest buildings in Kazan, contained only the bare necessities and lacked such basic teaching aids as maps and sometimes even chalk for the scarred blackboards. (Typically, the best-kept facility on campus was the immaculate, and rarely visited, Lenin Museum.) My Soviet colleagues marveled when I showed them color photographs of my private office at the University of Akron, complete with computer, private telephone, file cabinets, bookshelves, chairs for visitors, desklamp—things they can only dream about as they share desks in tiny offices and conduct consultations with students as crowds of people mill around.

Since I did very little research using Soviet sources (and read mainly newspapers and detective novels in Russian), I did not visit the university library very often. The place did not invite frequent use, however, as it was so poorly heated and insulated that students wore their coats while studying there, even before the onset of winter.

The library reflected traditional Soviet obsessions with controlling information. The user had access only to the card catalogue—there was no such thing as browsing the shelves. One had to find and order his or her book and wait for clerks to retrieve it, a pointless and time-consuming procedure.

Before *glasnost*, only authorized persons got access to certain materials that were considered politically suspect. One needed special permission, based on a clearly identified topic, to be admitted into back rooms and research archives where these supposedly political books and papers reposed. One professor told me he had gained access to such places, but had not been able to see all that he had wanted for his research. "They would say, 'No, that doesn't relate to your topic, I can't bring you that,' " he explained. In other words, clerks often made decisions they were not qualified to make and the whole procedure completely contravened the creative intellectual process.

Many of these practices are under reform today, of course. Even before the triumph of the pro-democracy movement, many revealing materials had become available to Soviet researchers under *glasnost*, including, for example, the Western journal *Slavic Review*, which features current research on all facets of Russian and Soviet history.

Perhaps even more stifling than the myriad bureaucratic impediments, Kazan State University, like others in the USSR, was burdened by an overwhelming provincialism that was the result of an almost total lack of mobility in Soviet society. Throughout Soviet history, citizens needed a *propiska*, or authorization, to live and work in a particular city, and could be arrested and deported for living in a city without the document. The *propiska*, a remnant of the tsarist autocracy that the Soviets perpetuated to control population patterns, was terminated in October 1991.

For years people in provincial cities like Kazan longed to live in Moscow, "the center," but were denied the opportunity and usually had to remain in their home cities. Leonia once told me about a friend of his, an exceptional case in which the man received a *propiska* to live in Moscow. Upon the man's arrival in the city, Leonia recalled with a laugh, "he said he wanted to kiss every locomotive in the train station, he was just so happy finally to be there."

As a result of this limited mobility, the overwhelming majority of the faculty at Kazan State was born, raised, and educated in Kazan. Whereas American academics only very rarely become faculty members at the institution where they receive their doctorate, precisely the opposite was true in the USSR. During my first week or two on campus, when I met new colleagues I would ask them where they were from and where they had received their degrees, until it finally dawned on me that the answer was almost always "Kazan, Kazan, Kazan."

A university should be a place of diversity and free thought, but Kazan was narrow, provincial, and hopelessly inbred. Cronyism encouraged not only pervasive abuses of the *blat* system, but academic corruption as well. At Kazan the practice of selling grades for favors was fairly widespread. "I know personally of several instances in which higher grades were exchanged for invitations to vacation in the Caucasus," one professor told me. Kazan had a lot of students from the south and the lure of a place to stay on the Black Sea coast, which a university professor might not otherwise be able to arrange or afford, could not fail to be tempting.

Less powerful inducements also worked. One morning I was walking in the hall with a Kazan State professor when two of her students appeared and handed her several packs of American cigarettes, which of course were not available in Kazan. "I don't know why they gave me these," she said, flashing me a nervous smile, but I felt sure they were a reward for a higher-than-deserved classroom evaluation.

On occasion professors pressure one another to give higher marks to a student who might be the son or daughter of a friend. "It's all done subtly, with euphemisms," one professor explained to me. "They'll say 'You don't want to hold this student back, do you? He's trying so hard, after all.' " My informant admitted that on occasion he had caved in to such pressure. "I've had many marginal students whom I've passed under this sort of pressure, but I've told people I am not comfortable with this and to please not ask me to do it again."

Cheating was also common at Kazan State University. Some students told me that when professors leave the room students quite openly cheat among themselves, unburdened by any sort of honor system or moral restraints. "They don't feel guilty," one student told me with a derisive laugh. "They only feel guilty if they get caught—guilty for their failure to get away with it." Even if caught in the act, students normally receive a wrist-slapping in the form of a verbal reprimand, or a warning. Rarely were there serious repercussions.

Normally, however, the method of evaluating students doesn't make it necessary to cheat. Rather than receiving a formal grade (in the USSR, 5 = A, 4 = B, etc.), many classes are offered *za schet* ("taken into account"), meaning the students will receive a check mark and a signature showing they have participated in the class, all of which is recorded in little books that they tote around at the end of each semester. The students seek out professors they call *avtomati*, that is those who can be counted upon *automatically* to sign the grade book without making an attempt to track whether the student had attended class or studied. This system lacks rigor and helps explain the erratic attendance and lack of interest students often display in university classes.

The West, God knows, is not immune to problems in higher education, but the corruption, disillusionment, and lack of a merit system made the situation far worse in Kazan and, presumably, the USSR as a whole. There seemed to be less order, fewer standards, a collapsing structure, all of which mirrored the general Soviet deterioration.

Much of what I observed was borne out by a survey taken by Soviet authorities themselves in spring 1991. As I learned upon my return home from an article in the *Chronicle of Higher Education* (Aug. 14, 1991), the survey of dozens of institutions of higher education, including all but three of the fifteen republics, produced depressing results. Nearly half of the students had no interest in their studies and no confidence that they would benefit from higher education, given the deterioration and political uncertainties of Soviet life. The survey also found that almost half of faculty members, embittered over low pay and limited upward mobility, wanted to leave higher education altogether. The Soviet official who conducted the survey concluded that the trends would lead to a "degradation of the nation" unless sweeping reforms were instituted.

During the year I spent in Kazan, the university chose a new rector, an aloof but capable man who had a small cadre of vice rectors who seemed to be committed to reform. "We have many problems," one of them told me, "much that must be changed. But it will be very difficult."

Even if officials in Kazan maintained their commitment to reform and showed a willingness to replace incompetent faculty and administrators, the desperate financial crisis in the country will prevent them from moving forward anytime soon. The university's budget has been slashed even as hyperinflation erodes buying power, all of which means fewer resources. One professor told me he was leaving for an important international conference in Moscow, the total cost of which—400 rubles—he would have to pay himself. That constituted a whole month's salary. "Before," he noted, "under the old prices, it would have cost me 150 rubles and the university would have paid for it." That was in 1991—by 1993 I'm sure it would have become all but impossible for him to make the trip at all.

Along the same lines, my friend Doog, the British linguist and a brilliant teacher, wanted to stay another year with the English Department, but the rector said the university could no longer afford to pay his modest salary. But how could they not afford to retain a native speaker, especially with knowledge of English crucial to a nation that is trying to broaden its ties with the West? One of Doog's sins had been to point out, in the most constructive manner possible, some of the deficiencies of the current practices at the university. Threatening the still-entrenched old guard by indicating the need for reform had been enough to get his contract terminated, though he did catch on at a nearby institute, which was delighted to have him.

The system of higher education, like society as a whole, will reform over time, though change will be slow and chaotic. The problems are so deeply ingrained that they will require at least a generation to root out. Meanwhile, many of the most capable people, precisely those who are needed to guide the society through its transformation, will continue to be victimized.

CHAPTER NINE

The Rebirth of Tatarstan

❦

KAZAN, WITH ITS MYRIAD factories, ubiquitous high-rise apartment buildings, crowded public transport, and empty store shelves, was in many respects a typical Soviet city.

What made the city unique, however, was its status as the capital of Tatarstan, the historic home of the Tatars, one of the largest ethnic minority groups in the former Soviet Union. About half of the city's more than one million residents, and 55 percent of the entire former autonomous republic's estimated 3.7 million people, are Tatars. Most of the rest are Russians, with a smattering of additional ethnic groups.

After years of relative calm in Kazan, *perestroika* and then political disintegration of the USSR ignited long dormant ethnic tensions between Tatars and Russians. So far, those tensions have been expressed nonviolently for the most part—some clashes have occurred but nothing like the conflicts in the Caucasus between Azerbaijanis and Armenians or Georgians and Ossetians. Nevertheless, the renascent Tatar-Russian tensions are unsettling to both groups, especially in Kazan where they must live and work together in roughly equal numbers.

When Ivan IV conquered and incorporated the khanate of Kazan in the sixteenth century, the Tatars, who themselves had come to the Volga region as conquerors in the thirteenth century, became the first non-Russian people with a state of their own to be incorporated into the Russian empire. Since then they have weathered russification, religious bias, and colonial exploitation, yet have preserved their language, religion, and culture to the point that Tatar nationalism is resurgent.

The designation of autonomous republic status dates to the time of Lenin. It offered a means of acknowledging the uniqueness of various minority groups without giving them autonomy in any real sense. "Tatarstan," or "Tataria," as some of the Tatar nationalists now refer to it, was wholly subservient to Moscow's economic, political, and social control throughout Soviet history since becoming an autonomous republic in 1920.

Throughout the republic, street signs are given in both Russian and Tatar. People may listen to all-Tatar radio and television stations as well. It was not at all unusual in Kazan to hear people conversing in Tatar, though most urban Tatars are fluent in Russian.

Before *perestroika*, ambitious Tatars tended to downplay their nationality and tried to blend in with the Russian majority as the best route to advancement. As a result of *glasnost*, however, Tatar nationalism reemerged and most Tatars today are proud to point out their nationality, traditions, and distinctiveness.

Radical independence groups, long kept closeted by the communist authorities, began to emerge under *perestroika*. The month I arrived in Kazan, in October 1990, a group called *Ittifaq*, the National Independence Party, held demonstrations in Freedom Square, where a large crowd of people, mostly men wearing the black Tatar skullcap, chanted "Allah is great" and called for Tatarstan to be an independent homeland for all Tatars, including some five million spread across the USSR as a result of the "Tatar diaspora"—what is viewed as a forced migration of Tatars away from their homeland. Many Tatars see themselves as the Palestinians of the former Soviet Union. They have called for an independent Tatarstan, use of the Tatar language in schools, Islamic education, and days off on the Muslim holy Friday instead of Sunday.

Before the collapse of the USSR in the wake of the failed August coup, there was much more support, at least among Tatars, for the idea of making Tatarstan a union republic. Such a designation would, in theory, equate it with the Russian Republic, Belorussia, Ukraine, and the other fifteen union republics that once constituted the USSR.

"Why shouldn't we be a union republic?" demanded my friend Ildar, a Tatar and university physics professor. "Why must everything be decided in Moscow? Even the paper upon which my diploma is written must be signed in Moscow. Why is it so?"

But, I protested, Tatarstan was far from the only autonomous republic in the USSR. What if each of the twenty autonomous republics (sixteen of which are in the Russian republic) demanded union republic status?

"So what?" responded Ildar. "Russia is the size of your country. You have fifty states in your country, the power is spread out, and is it so terrible for you? We want only the same thing."

Advocates of real autonomy for Tatarstan cite economic motives as well as political and historic ones. The Tatar Autonomous Republic was the second largest oil producer in the former USSR and contains substantial industries, including major aircraft works and the Kamaz truck plant, which produced 25 percent of the country's vehicles. Those who want greater autonomy for Tatarstan—including some Russians—complain that they contribute more than they receive from the union with Russia, and pay high taxes as well.

The Tatar parliament reflected the new assertiveness by officially declaring the "sovereignty" of Tatarstan in August 1990. A region-wide referendum early in 1992 produced majority support for outright independence of Tatarstan, which would make it the equal of Russia, Ukraine, or any of the other independent states of the new Commonwealth. Boris Yeltsin and the Russian government have rejected the notion of an independent Tatarstan, however.

The local government has also declared Tatar an official language of the republic, making it equal with Russian, and angering Russians who fear that their children will be forced to learn Tatar. Even more unsettling to many Russians, the crescent moon and star of Islam were mounted on the fourteenth century church spire across the courtyard from the local Supreme Soviet and government office buildings.

Although there is little evidence of any widespread Islamic fundamentalism, Tatars point out with pride that Kazan is the northernmost outpost of Islam. Under *perestroika* and subsequently, Muslim mosques have been refurbished and reopened and many Tatars now attend services regularly. I dropped in on one service where the men knelt on their prayer rugs on one floor while the women, kept segregated under Islamic tradition, had to hear the incantations of the mullah piped through a sound system into the basement below.

While most Tatars I met did not attend mosque and showed little interest in Islamic fundamentalism, the radicals were vocal. At the Freedom Square rally, some Tatar demonstrators carried signs protesting intermarriage between Tatars and Russians, which they feared would undermine the Tatars as a distinctive group. Such activities alarmed the local Russian population, some of whom circulated unconfirmed reports that the Tatar protesters carried signs calling for infanticide of babies born of mixed marriages.

Although roughly one-third of the marriages in Kazan consist of a union between a Tatar and a Russian, there is still widespread opposition to the practice. I knew one couple in whose case the mother of the Tatar man refused for several years to acknowledge the existence of his Russian wife. Only when the first child was born did she resign herself to the mixed union. Another Tatar woman, a close friend of mine, explained to me that she found it difficult to warm up to her brother's wife, who was Russian, and added that had her father been alive he would have vigorously opposed the marriage.

I got to know one Tatar radical, a university dean named Ilduce Rajirev, about 50 years old, who advocated Tatar independence and personally opposed intermarriage between Tatars and Russians. According to a mutual acquaintance, he had forbidden one of his two sons from dating a Russian woman and banished the young man from the house when he refused to follow his father's wishes.

Rajirev and his wife, both of whom had jet-black hair and Oriental features typical of the Tatars, joined me as dinner guests at the home of a Russian colleague one night shortly after I arrived in Kazan. He spoke with great pride about Tatar history and culture throughout the evening, citing the names of famous Tatars who lived in other countries of the world. "Even in your America," he noted, "there are many of our people."

Rajirev himself was a Communist, a party member who still had not resigned in 1990, as had more than half the party members affiliated with the university. To him the enemy of the aspirations of the Tatars was not Soviet communism but Russian chauvinism. For that reason, Rajirev, like many Tatar nationalists I met, preferred

Gorbachev to Yeltsin, whom they viewed as a traditional Russian chauvinist. After all, it was Ivan IV, a Russian, who had sacked Kazan, not the communists, who at least had given the Tatars designation as an autonomous republic.

To many Tatars, Yeltsin, who gained popularity partly on his appeals to the idea of an independent Russia, embodies the historic domination of Tatarstan by the Russians. Yeltsin has confirmed their suspicions by repeatedly declaring that Tatarstan must remain a part of the Russian Republic.

Rajirev, however, wanted to turn back the clock to the political realities of the first half of the sixteenth century (but not to the twelfth century!), before Ivan the Terrible conquered the Tatars. "Our goal is total independence," he told me.

Wasn't it unrealistic, I asked, to try to carve out an independent state in the heart of Russia? Wouldn't the result be violent ethnic dissension? Rajirev shrugged as if to say "Maybe so, but we want our independence."

The Russian hostess who had invited us for the evening meal counted the Tatar couple as close friends but, as for most Russians in Kazan, talk of Tatar independence made her nervous. "They are obsessed with the nationalities question," she told me later. "Other than that, they are wonderful people."

Rajirev represented the most radical position—total independence—which many Tatars, not to mention Russians, consider unrealistic.

I slowly mastered the political geography of the Russian-Tatar conflict, but I couldn't really comprehend the distinctiveness of the Tatars as a people until I made a trip for a weekend wedding ceremony in a remote Tatar village in March 1991.

A good friend of mine from the university, a beautiful dark-haired Tatar woman named Alsue, who spoke fluent English, invited me to her home for dinner, where I met her husband, Ravil, also a Tatar, and their two delightful children, eight-year-old Icylu and five-year-old Irat. Alsue always served delicious homemade Tatar specialties like *ishpishmak*, steaming triangular shaped meat, potato, and onion pies. Ravil, thoroughly russified, always did his best to keep the vodka flowing.

Before I left one night, Alsue mentioned that a childhood friend of hers, a doctor living in Kazan, was getting married in their native village, about fifty miles north of the city, and that while she couldn't attend herself, Ravil was going and I was welcome to tag along with him and the children. I promptly accepted.

Ravil and I met at the downtown wedding chapel in Kazan, a spacious modern building where couples routinely were married and photographed under the hammer-and-sickle insignia and a giant portrait of Lenin. The actual ceremony is little more than a brief formality, with the real emotion and celebration coming later.

After the ceremony, about twenty of us gathered ourselves for the trip into the countryside in a lumbering, rusted-out, half-size bus, which shuddered under the full impact of every pothole on the pock-marked streets of Kazan. Ravil and I stood side to side inside the bus with the Tatar wedding party, all strangers to me, as we lurched across the city to an apartment complex. There, to my horror, I realized we were picking up still more people for the two-hour trip into the countryside.

Several men proceeded to construct crude benches by placing sawhorses and planks in the aisle of the bus to accommodate the mass of people, who would ensure that we violated Soviet law about maximum occupancy of a single vehicle. I actually looked forward to the perverse experience of riding into the countryside jammed together with strangers in this deathtrap of a vehicle, but Ravil used the *blat* of my Americanism and persuaded a couple who had their own car to take the two of us and his two children with them.

The ride was the kind of disorganized farce that only the Soviets could engineer while still managing to have a good time. At one point the bus and the two cars got separated and I looked on in amazement as the groom and other tuxedoed men flagged down cars going in the opposite direction on the other side of the high-speed road in order to ask drivers if they'd seen our bus anywhere up ahead. I was sure they were all crazy—after all, there were lots of buses on the road and a driver coming the opposite way would only have a few seconds to see one—but then a truck driver said, yes, he'd just seen an old white bus full of people twenty or thirty minutes before. So, wearing big grins, the groom and his best men trotted back across the street and we all piled back into the cars and sped off to catch up with the bus.

Once our caravan was reunited, we stopped off at a beautifully ornate wooden museum honoring the famous Tatar poet Gobdullah Tukayev. We viewed the original work of the man known as the "Tatar Pushkin," in part because of his poetic talent but also because he, like the great Russian poet, died at an early age. Before his death from tuberculosis at age 27, Tukayev wrote several volumes of poetry, started a Tatar newspaper in Arabic, and became a celebrated man of letters in the years preceding the revolution. He had been a controversial figure among the Tatars because he rejected the traditional robes and skullcap for a modern suit and tie.

As we filed through the museum, I realized that my new Tatar friends were honoring the distinctiveness of their culture on a day of celebration. The guide conducted the museum tour in Tatar and all present were Tatars who spoke the native language.

When we finally pulled into the tiny village, it was almost dusk on a cold winter night. In keeping with custom, a greeting party had been assembled in the cold to throw open a high wooden gate, allowing the bus and cars to pull up next to the home where the evening's festivities would take place. As I got out of our car, Ravil grabbed my arm and pointed ahead to the wedding party.

As the bride prepared to step out of their car, the ebullient crowd closed in on her and one woman placed a pillow on the wet ground for the bride, who wore a traditional flowing white gown, to step upon so that her purity would not be sullied by the dirty ground. At the moment that she stood on the pillow, another matron shoved a spoonful of butter and honey into her mouth, which she swallowed as everyone clapped and cheered. According to Tatar tradition, the concoction ensured that the new marriage would be rich, sweet, and lasting.

Ravil and I dropped off our things, as well as his two kids, at the home of Alsue's uncle, where we would be staying, and proceeded to the wedding party. Like most of the village structures, the building where the party was held was made of wood with dried mud and grass stuffed between the logs. A typical Tatar home, it was painted in bright colors with contrasting stripes and ornate trim around windowsills and doorframes.

Tables and chairs had been neatly organized inside to accommodate the forty or fifty of us who crammed into the main room to commence a celebration that lasted eight hours. The bride and groom introduced their families and friends, after which we ate our salad dishes, drank the first toasts, and then adjourned for smoking and dancing out in the cold, where speakers blared and floodlights shone under the black winter sky.

We returned for the next course, more toasts and speeches, and listened to humorous musical numbers and Tatar folk ballads performed by two silver-toothed young men who had grown up in the village with the groom. They played an accordion and had the whole room clapping rhythmically and smiling. The occasion was so festive that it made no difference to me that all the festivities were conducted in Tatar and I understood none of the words.

Whenever we moved outside, a new circle of villagers would materialize near the big open gate to look on, smiling happily and enjoying a rare main event in the tiny village. Each time we went back inside, a hard-working group of women had removed all the dirty dishes, replaced the empty vodka bottles, and readied the next course. Supplies of food and alcohol had been accumulated for weeks in anticipation of the reception and the village women had obviously been cooking for hours, if not indeed days. The *defitsit* couldn't be allowed to undermine an occasion such as this.

In keeping with tradition, balloons containing handwritten commands were floated around the room and burst open with knives, forks, and ink pens. Whomever they landed closest to had to read the note and follow the command while the entire group looked on. Inevitably, one of the burst balloons landed by me and the note called on me to give a toast.

"*Koshmar* (what a nightmare!)" I said, standing at my place at the table as fifty Tatars looked up at me with eager smiles. Speaking in Russian, I thanked them for inviting me to the wedding and declared that the bride and groom made a beautiful couple, as indeed they did. I sat down to a big round of applause and Ravil whispered "*Molodets*" ("well done").

The Tatars seemed delighted to have an American present and the bride and groom told me they were personally honored. I took pictures with my automatic camera, whose whirring film advance mechanism proved so fascinating that the camera was passed around the room for people to admire. While Ravil was on one side of me, on the other side sat a very bright, grinning fifteen-year-old relative of the groom, who was suitably impressed when I demonstrated all the blades, the corkscrew, the tweezers, and even the toothpick on my Swiss Army knife.

After we ate our main course and sang a few more songs, attendants passed around a tray upon which we laid money as gifts while making a final brief statement of good wishes for the new couple. It was 3 A.M. before the final round of dancing and singing ended outside in the snow. Ravil and I shuffled home, laughing and comparing observations about the relative attractiveness of the women at the party.

When we returned to the uncle's house I discovered that the only bed in the living room had been reserved for me while Ravil and Alsue's uncle, whose name was Gennia, insisted on sleeping alongside on mats on the wooden floor. After only a pretense of trying to talk them out of it, I collapsed onto the bed.

The day and night activities had left me exhausted, but Ravil's children came bursting into the living room full of energy before 7 A.M., rousing us from the fog. Somehow I managed to tug on clothes and stagger to the breakfast table, where Alsue's aunt, Gulnure, placed a steaming bowl of gruel—and a shotglass of vodka before me.

"Well, did you choose a girl last night?" she asked brightly.

"Huh?," I stammered, barely comprehending, but when it became evident that I had failed to do so, she and Gennia seemed disappointed.

I tried to push the vodka away, as my stomach churned. "No, no, you must drink it," said the uncle, shoving the shotglass back under my nose, his gold teeth flashing a big smile, "you will feel much better." Ravil, who felt about like I did, nodded and picked up his glass.

Finding myself dragged along by the Soviets, as usual, I drained a shotglass of vodka at 7 A.M. on Sunday morning. The truth was, however, that in moments I did indeed feel much better, which I interpreted as an ominous sign of creeping sovietization.

After breakfast followed by a short period of sitting around groaning, Aunt Gulnure announced that our *bania* was prepared. It was not the first time I had taken one of the long, sometimes unbearably hot steam baths, which the Soviets cherished and praised for their salubrious effect on body and soul.

As with many Tatar homes—in Kazan as well as the countryside—the *bania*, housed in a separate wooden building just a few steps out the back door, compensated for the lack of indoor plumbing. I met many Tatars in Kazan who habitually started their winter days with a quick visit to the outdoor privy, followed by a long steam bath, all culminated by an ice cold bucket of water over the head, or a quick romp in the snow. It was, they explained, the lightning transition from intense heat to bitter cold that ensured good health.

On this occasion, the three of us lounged in the *bania* for about two hours, which for Ravil and Gennia was merely routine. To cope with the intense heat, I took more than the usual number of breaks, stepping outside into the cold in my towel for deep breaths and to let the beads of sweat begin to turn to ice.

Soviets wash, rub, and brush themselves meticulously in the *bania*, the men unselfconsciously soaping each other's arms and backs. The one practice I couldn't abide, however, was the routine whipping of each other with a three-foot long bundle of branches, *berioza* leaves, taken from supposedly medicinal branches of the birch tree. The first time I tried it in Kazan I got welts on my thighs from lying on the overheated cedar boards while my back, which broke out in tiny hives, was being whacked repeatedly with a bundle of wet branches. I decided that going native had its limitations, though my Soviet friends swore by the practice and whipped each other vigorously for minutes on end.

Soviets, seldom in a hurry to do anything, were happy to spend the better part of a day in the *bania* if the occasion allowed. On a weekend the usual practice was to take some beer and a few snacks and make a day of bathing, snacking, and conversation.

"There, now," said Gennia as we towelled off that Sunday afternoon, "*that* was a real *bania*." After the long bath and a huge village lunch of hearty soup, salads, and fresh meat pies baked in an earthen stove, I felt almost totally refreshed.

After lunch, I joined Ravil and his uncle on a tour of the village collective farm (*kolkhoz*), where Gennia was an administrator. We walked across the snowy fields in high black boots with the obligatory fur hats perched on our heads, our faces chapped from the cold wind. As we approached a group of outbuildings, a long-legged brown hare bolted from the brush and skittered across the icy hillside.

When we arrived at a large aluminum sheeted barn, Gennia explained that the *kolkhoz*, which typically specializes in one major agricultural activity, had raised rabbits before, but a new director had come in a few years ago and—on orders from Moscow, of course—shifted operations to cattle. Gennia was happy about that since his family, unlike those in Kazan, now always had plenty of fresh meat.

As we stepped inside the barn, healthy looking cattle on short chains stood in rows, while farm women wearing baggy dresses, traditional white scarves, and jackets forked hay into the trough at one end and scooped up manure at the other. (Bringing to mind experiences on my parents' Kentucky farm, I reflected that cow dung smelled the same, irrespective of the continent of origin.)

Gennia introduced me to one of the women workers, all of whom seemed over fifty, and she nodded and said she already learned of my presence in the village. "You know," she added, flashing a big grin, accented by a few missing teeth, "you are the only American who has ever stood on this spot. Let me at least touch you," she said, reaching out to pinch my jacket, as we all laughed. It was true: no one recalled an American ever being in their village before. I felt a little bit like Neil Armstrong.

Having finished our tour and eaten a little supper, we dropped into the town's "cultural center" for a depressing glimpse of the underside of village life. The ebullience of the night before had given way to blaring hard rock music, drunkenness, and the dreariness of a Soviet Saturday night with nowhere to go and nothing to do.

A crumbling beige concrete building housed the cultural center, which contained nothing cultural, but was the only place that the twenty or thirty teenagers lining the walls could go. A few danced in the dark without enthusiasm on the dusty wooden floorboards as we made our way through the first room beyond the direct flow of the pounding speakers. The next room was lit, but also virtually barren except for a gigantic, lifesize portrait of Lenin, which hung slightly askew on the cracked walls.

One bombed-out youth bounced bleary-eyed from group to group like a wound-up top. He was unable to speak, but afraid to stand still. The silver-toothed accordion player of the night before saw us and strode over to grab my hand, clinging to it while he spoke too rapidly for me to follow him with the music blaring in the background, spraying me in the face with emphatic, vodka-laced pronouncements.

Ravil noticed my discomfort as I gently pulled away. We soon made our way out the door and into the relief of the cold outside air. Gennia was as discomfited as I. "You hear that music," he said, shaking his head and gesticulating. "Before we had our *own* music and dances and now they only listen to your [Western] rock music."

As we continued the conversation back inside Gennia's home, it was clear that the erosion of his native culture deeply disturbed this 45-year-old Tatar villager. "Look at him," he said, jabbing his thumb accusingly toward Ravil, "his kids don't even speak our native language. It's the very worst thing," he said, pounding on the table.

I recalled earlier that morning when Gennia had tried to speak to Icylu and Irat in Tatar, but they had twisted away uncomfortably, only understanding fragments of the language, leaving the older man visibly upset. His own two teenage sons, healthy village youngsters who were trying to grow their first mustaches, understood Russian but declined to speak it. In response to direct questions from me, they would respond in Tatar to Ravil, who translated. "They're just not very comfortable speaking Russian," Ravil explained.

Although Ravil himself was fluent in Tatar, he and Alsue saw no pressing need to teach their children the language, but instead were teaching them English. I recalled seeing a few weeks earlier a plastic set of brightly colored letters from the Roman alphabet the kids could use to form words in their tiny, one-bedroom Kazan apartment. They already knew several words and giggled eagerly when I spoke English with them, in sharp contrast to the way they responded to Uncle Gennia.

Ravil confirmed that the children themselves didn't have any enthusiasm for learning Tatar. "They need only Russian at school and we teach them some English at home. We don't have the time or energy to do much more. I feel guilty and ashamed in front of our people," he added, then flashing a grin, "but not too much."

Whereas Gennia, product of the previous generation and still leading a traditional village lifestyle, found the erosion of Tatar language and culture upsetting, Ravil, younger, urban, and influenced by Western culture, accepted the change as inevitable. "It's an irreversible process," he explained. "Our people are spread out all over the country and more and more assimilated all the time. I suppose that happens in every country, including your immigrants in America. Still, it is difficult for the Tatar people."

Fatigue soon overwhelmed our seminar on culture and linguistics and we all went to sleep early. The next morning we said good-bye to the family, a scene I recall almost painfully as one of the myriad occasions when I struggled to express my thanks in a foreign language to people who had never met me before yet had taken me into their homes, given me everything they had, treating me like family. I never felt up to the task of closing out these encounters, which frequently aroused a welling of emotion that surprised no one more than myself. As we left, Gennia gave Ravil several kilograms of fresh meat in a bag to take home.

Before boarding an outrageously crowded public bus, which reeked with exhaust fumes, Ravil and I stopped off at his wife's grandmother's house for a visit. As we trudged down the icy street to *babushka's* wooden cabin, a one-horse sleigh trotted by and Ravil hailed the driver. The bearded man nodded at Ravil's request and we piled onto the sleigh, gaining a perch as the old farm horse glanced around with a noticeable lack of enthusiasm.

After all the years that had passed since I first sang "Jingle Bells" in grade school, I found myself grinning at the realization that I was actually riding to grandmother's house in a one-horse open sleigh—albeit in Russia.

As we trotted down the meandering village road and across a small wooden bridge, the villagers, who all seemed to know who I was, looked on and waved while working in their yards or drawing water from the outdoor spigots, which were wrapped in layers of stiff cloth to keep them from freezing.

Once we had warmed our hands over *babushka's* iron stove, we sat down for a chat before catching the bus. *Babushka*, 85 years old, had lived in the village her whole life. Despite the impediments of conversation—she spoke only in Tatar to Ravil, who translated for me into Russian—she proved to be a fascinating source of oral history and I regretted that we couldn't spend more time with her.

For months I had been meeting Soviets who were continually grousing about their lives and the deterioration of their society, but *babushka* had seen far worse times. Indeed, she had been witness, and victim, to the entire revolutionary experience.

Her grandfather, a wealthy peasant (*kulak*) before 1917, had been imprisoned after the Revolution and died from exposure and starvation while lying in chains in a watery cellar. Her parents were also well-to-do, but died early of illness, leaving *babushka* and her five brothers and sisters to be brought up by relatives.

She recalled the collectivization of agriculture in the 1930s, when Stalin's men had come and regimented the workers, forcing the people to toil day and night in the fields and seizing their private plots. One of her three children, Gennia's sister, had been born while *babushka* worked in the fields. She had simply put down her pitchfork and gone into labor in a hayfield.

Unable to bear the strain of life on the collective, her husband stole away from the village—and from *babushka*—and later fought in Eastern Europe in World War II. He returned after the war and died in 1983. While he was gone, *babushka* had no choice but to work and raise her five children by herself.

The war years were the worst. She had to work from three in the morning until nine at night and left her small children at home, with some food laid out, to care for themselves. There was no one to watch them because every hand was needed for the war effort. Once a week she would walk to a nearby town—a 30- or 40-mile roundtrip—to deliver a huge sack of grain. She did the work of a village horse because all of them had been taken away for the war effort.

In the late war years there was famine in the village and *babushka* stole 800 grams of bread in an attempt to feed her children. She was arrested and sentenced to prison for eight years, of which she served three before being released. Her children all survived by living with her older sister in the village.

Babushka relayed all of this as she sat calmly, hands on knees over her loose print dress, her white hair covered by the traditional peasant head scarf, a contented smile on her face. After listening to her, the problems of contemporary Soviet society seemed mundane. I had many questions I wanted to ask, but we had to catch the bus. I promised myself I would come back to the village in springtime, but never did.

Babushka, speaking only in Tatar and recalling the horrors of Stalinism, represented the isolated rural past. Although many people perpetuate the traditional village lifestyle—Gennia and his family on one side, the hard-drinking youth in the cultural center on the other—Ravil, Alsue, and their family have left the traditional society behind.

Proud but not obsessed about their Tatar nationality, they were not much interested in undoing Ivan IV's conquest of Kazan. Forward and Western looking, they studied English and won the envy of many of their Kazan friends when Alsue became Soviet Education Project Coordinator for the National Audubon Society. Her job, translating Audubon books and leaflets into Russian, gave her the opportunity to move to the northeastern United States with her family. They have permission to stay for three years, but intend to make the move permanent.

While Alsue and Ravil have put the nationalities question far behind, it remains to be worked out in Kazan. Even before the failed August coup and the total collapse of Soviet authority, many of my friends and acquaintances in Kazan shook their heads apprehensively when the nationalities question surfaced. "But it seems so calm to me," I would protest, having seen no evidence of extremely high tensions or impending violence.

"Yes, it's calm now," they would reply, "but tensions can erupt very easily."

They were right. After I returned to the United States, Leonia wrote that another demonstration in Kazan's Freedom Square had resulted in a clash that left several people injured, including two policemen.

Now that Soviet authority has disintegrated, the Communist Party and the central government in Moscow can no longer serve as a buffer between Tatar nationalists and traditional Russian chauvinism. As a result, Tatar radicals have stepped up their call for an independent state. What's good enough for the Baltic states, Ukraine and Byelorus, they say, is good enough for them. The only impediment, they charge, is Russian imperialism, of which the distrusted Yeltsin remains the prime example. All of this is exacerbated, of course, by the severe economic crisis, which leaves people increasingly angry and receptive to reactionary solutions and the illusive appeal of demagogues.

I doubt that the Tatar radicals will achieve enough of a following to effectively challenge Russia's suzerainty, but nothing can be ruled out these days in the former USSR. Based on my experience in the Tatar republic, most Tatars care more about economic security and fulfilling their potential as individuals than about the Tatar-Russian conflict. The high rate of intermarriage between Russians and Tatars in Kazan ideally will preclude the type of violent conflict that has characterized relations between Armenians and Azerbaijanis, or Georgians and Ossetians, in the Caucasus.

Ultimately, however, the fate of Tatarstan, like everything else in the former USSR, is likely to remain highly unstable for some time.

CHAPTER TEN

Men, Women, Sex, and the Family

MY FRIEND, call him Nikolai, and I were walking from the tram stop to the apartment of another friend, who together with his wife had invited us to dinner.

Since I had never met the man's wife, I asked Nikolai what she was like. "She is a very good person and very attractive," he said. In fact, added Nikolai, he had just had an affair with her.

"You what?" I exclaimed. "Does her husband know? Aren't you nervous about being entertained in their home?"

"No, he probably doesn't know about it," Nikolai replied, "or if he does he hasn't said anything." He shrugged. "Her husband is very preoccupied with his work and she is not very satisfied with him."

Nikolai didn't seem to think any of this particularly remarkable. In fact, the woman, married for thirteen years, told him that he was the first man she had had an affair with, but that most of her friends had affairs and she was beginning to feel strange for *not* having taken a *lubovnik* (a lover) during the course of her marriage.

We proceeded to the apartment and all enjoyed a pleasant evening of eating, conversation, and dancing. There was no discernible tension in the atmosphere.

Over the course of my ten months in the USSR, I noticed that attitudes and practices about sex and the family diverged from those in the West. I found that while Soviets didn't necessarily do a lot of talking about sex, they were somehow less uptight about it, generally more promiscuous, and usually more direct about initiating sexual activity than many Americans.

Extramarital affairs, while far from uncommon in the West, were more prevalent in Soviet society, particularly among people in their mid-forties and under. The Russian word *guliat'*, which literally means to "take a stroll," is the common reference to "stepping out" on a marriage.

Although there is a high level of promiscuity in Soviet society, I did meet scores of apparently monogamous couples and lots of single people, especially women, who had no sex lives at all. Many people, no doubt a majority, viewed monogamy or abstinence rather than promiscuity as the appropriate approach to sexual relations.

But there were many others, both single and married, who evidenced no moral—and certainly no religious—qualms about promiscuousness, including extramarital liaisons. Rather, as in the case of Nikolai, they accepted such practices matter of factly.

Soviets often looked outside their marriages for sexual satisfaction in part because they had gotten married for utilitarian purposes rather than out of sexual attraction or "true love."

"I am very fond of my husband and he is a good father," one Soviet woman told me, "but I do not really love him. We did not get married for this reason."

The actual reason for their decision to marry was as mundane as it was common. She and her husband got married as a means of escaping the homes of their parents for an apartment of their own. The state would provide an apartment for married couples, but would not do so for single people because of the acute housing shortage.

Only under extraordinary circumstances can a single person receive an apartment of his or her own in the USSR. In all my time there, I can recall only one single woman, and no single men, who lived alone. The overwhelming majority of single persons, including some in their thirties, forties, and fifties, still lived with their parents.

Many of these people are desperate to quit their parents' homes. When I left the USSR in July 1990, my friend Lilia and her four-year-old son were living with her mother, with whom she had an increasingly stormy relationship. Lilia's husband had died in a tragic automobile accident two years before and she desperately feared going through life without a male partner or an apartment of her own.

I got a letter three months later in which Lilia informed me that she was getting married to a man, fourteen years older, whom she had just met. He was a good man, she said. He had decent work, a nice apartment, and was willing to take on the child.

She said nothing of love, sexual attractiveness, or even his personality. These simply were not relevant to her decision to marry him.

In Soviet society it was socially acceptable for men to pursue relationships with women twelve to fifteen years younger. I, at age thirty-five, dated two women during my ten months in the USSR. One was 23, the other 21.

No one thought anything of it, least of all the women themselves. "You are the perfect age for girls my age," the 21-year-old woman, a "Tatarka" (Tatar female) named Rimma, once told me. When I asked her why, she shrugged and smiled as if to say "that's just the way it is." I often told Soviet friends that in the West most women in their early twenties went out with men more or less their own age and many considered it almost perverse to date men twelve to fifteen years older. Invariably my Soviet friends would wrinkle their noses in consternation and ask, "But why?"

I couldn't really give them a good answer any more than I can explain why the younger Soviet women preferred to date older men (and not just Americans). Perhaps it was because many of the younger men are immature and not well established in a material or social sense.

Rimma's mother always warmly welcomed me into their apartment and would vacate the living room in order to give us privacy. She did not seem to think I was robbing the cradle, though she feared I might ask her daughter to marry me and she didn't want that, even if I was, by their standards, a rich American. Rimma and I actually liked each other a lot, but we drifted apart and in the end she went back to her former boyfriend, who treated her badly.

By that time I had already cooled relations with the other woman I had dated, Gulia, whom I sensed was pushing me toward commitment. On a couple of occasions, when I told her directly that I wasn't planning on marriage, she shot back: "What makes you think I want to marry an American? You all think that you're so important." I accepted her rebuke, but in the end I had to doubt Gulia's honesty when I heard, after returning home in the fall of 1991, that she had come to the United States on a three-week visit at the invitation of some American students she'd met and had married a man whom she'd never seen before. Gulia, I understand, is now an American citizen living in the Washington area.

I had many female friends who did not treat me any differently simply because I was a passport-carrying representative of the "American Boy, American Joy" fantasy, but there were of course many who did.

One of the most personally wrenching cases was a Tatar woman in her mid-thirties, Delara, who I thought was merely an acquaintance but who ended up professing her undying love.

Before she let me in on her feelings, Delara had merely been one of the handful of people who had faithfully attended all my lectures at the university. I appreciated the interest these people displayed and made it a point to interact with them whenever possible.

I first learned that Delara had developed a romantic attachment when she showed up one evening at the train station to see me off for a trip to Moscow. She came into my train compartment before the train pulled out and presented me with a bulging sack of food—sandwiches, fruit, and hard-boiled eggs. I didn't even know how she knew I was leaving town for the weekend.

I was so surprised that I didn't know what to say. Meanwhile, she took as encouraging the absence of any other female seeing me off at the station. Before the train pulled out she waited outside my window shivering in the cold, staring up at me like a homeless puppy, while I paced in my compartment in confusion.

After I returned from Moscow, a mutual friend told me that Delara was absolutely in love with me and that I had to make it clear to her that I was not interested.

Cravenly, I sought to avoid just such a conversation until Delara cornered me one day at the university and confessed that for five months she had been deeply in love with me. Her feelings were so strong, she said, that she had consulted an occultist for guidance. "From that first day five months ago I have felt the waves rolling from me to you," she said.

Perhaps it's an ethnocentric judgment but I've already said, and firmly believe, that many Soviets can't take a hint. One must be blunt. So I said: "Delara, you have to understand that I *do not* have the same waves coming to me from you that you seem to be getting from me."

"You are lying," she replied, her eyes blazing. "The occultist said that the waves come in pairs. If I am getting them from you then you must be getting them from me. Don't you *feel* it?"

No, I told her, I didn't feel it and I didn't think she should rely on the words of some occultist, who was probably a quack. "How can you not believe in the laws of the cosmos?" replied Delara, an English speaker. "I know you have more books on such things than we do. You must know all about it."

This went on for some time until I suggested that maybe we ought to cut down on our contact with one another since this was proving painful for her. "No, don't shut me off," she said, "or something terrible will happen to you. When I myself tried before to forget about my love for you, I became very ill."

She finally left, weeping. Delara and I remained friends during my last two months in the USSR, but we spoke no further about love and the laws of the cosmos. Despite her superstitions, she was an intelligent and successful professional woman but had grown desperately lonely and frustrated by what she and her society perceived as her failure to find a husband and have a family. She seemed to prefer Westerners, however, as I'm told I was the third one she'd supposedly fallen in love with.

The traditions associated with Islamic culture, including the strong subordination of women to men, placed much greater pressure on the Tatar women like Delara than on Russians. One young Tatar woman, a bright and articulate computer programmer in her early twenties, spoke of the constraints to remain chaste before marriage.

She had finally begun to have sex with her boyfriend, which at first caused her considerable anguish until she began to enjoy the newfound activity. After conferring privately with her sister, she concluded that, even though she wasn't married, "It was time for me to begin having sex." But she still had to contend with her mother, who sometimes grilled her about her activities and kept trying to set her up with Tatar men she didn't care for so that she would get married and not cause a scandal.

Friends told me of another Tatar woman who had remained a virgin until marriage, but her husband refused to believe her because she had not bled after their first intercourse. Such attitudes, relatively rare now, used to be more common in generations and centuries past, when Tatar brides could be rejected for not "proving" their chastity and when village men sometimes proudly hung bloody sheets outside for all to see the day after the wedding ceremony.

Both Tatar men and women, at least in some families, felt pressure to choose a fellow Tatar as a marriage partner. Once married, however, some Tatar men, to a greater degree than Russians, I thought, subscribed to a double standard whereby having extramarital affairs was almost a badge of honor. If their wives did the same thing, however, it was considered treacherous, sinful, and grounds for a beating and divorce.

Single women in their mid- to late-twenties and thirties suffered most from the inequities of male-female relations in Russia. These women are branded—as early as *age 25*—as a *staraia devka*: an "old maid."

I met many such women in their late twenties and early thirties who were frustrated, desperate, or simply resigned to the situation. Some of these women still hoped for marriage but at the same time resigned themselves to affairs with usually much older, married men. Others had no sexual relationships at all.

One woman, Lena, 34 years old and never married, had a constant stream of older married men visiting her, bringing over chickens, flowers, and other gifts in an effort to get her in bed. She lived with her mother, who vacated the house once or twice a week to accommodate her daughter's sexual privacy. Lena's only regular lover was a married man who had given her and her mother one thousand rubles the year before so that they could go on vacation together to Vladivostok. (She had liked him a lot.)

While Lena still found her love life fundamentally unfulfilling, because it did not include a husband and children, she at least seemed to enjoy having several men pursuing her. I met other women who were far more frustrated.

Many women found the inequities and frustrations of male-female relations so overwhelming that they resigned themselves to having no intimacy with men at all. One of these women was my friend Guselle, a dark-haired, attractive philosophy professor at a Kazan institute. She had been disappointed in a couple of relationships and had decided, at age 31, that fate had determined that she would be single and alone for life.

"Our men are worthless," she told me, "they only think of themselves. I don't have anything to do with men," she added, staring off into space after a trail of blue cigarette smoke.

Guselle had devoted most of her emotional energy to her work and acting as mother to her sister, nine years younger, after their parents had both died when she was a teenager. They had a large apartment, though it had no hot water, and barely enough money to cover their monthly expenses. "It's been very hard, of course," she told me.

Guselle worried a great deal about her sister, Assia, who had long been dating Anton, a good-humored and intelligent young professional. Guselle liked but did not fully trust Anton, whom Assia wanted to marry. "He says they are engaged but he doesn't say when they will get married," Guselle told me. "This is typical of our men."

On my last visit to their apartment in Kazan in June, a delighted Guselle told me that Assia and Anton had decided to get married. I gave them a wedding present and we drank a toast to the occasion. Later they sent me black and white wedding photographs.

"What made you decide to get married, Anton?" I asked innocently after our toast, whereupon Guselle burst out laughing and Assia and Anton quickly joined in. Guselle finally explained that the two had decided to get married because Assia was pregnant. I was the only one who was even remotely embarrassed: after all, pregnancy was a logical reason for matrimony.

One of the most blatant failures of the Soviet system has been its inability to provide the populace with readily available and reliable forms of birth control. If a planned society can accomplish anything, it ought to do that.

After discussing this issue with scores of men and women, however, it was clear that the most common form of birth control was the notoriously unreliable rhythm method. Condoms are expensive and only sometimes available in drugstores, though most men don't want to have anything to do with them anyway. Diaphragms come in three set sizes, if a woman is lucky enough to find them, and there is no spermicidal cream. A birth control pill exists in the former USSR, but is also difficult to obtain and not nearly as reliable as Western varieties.

"Men don't care about" the risks of pregnancy, one young woman told me. "They just want to do it and the rest is the woman's problem. Let her worry about it." Some men, like Anton, will marry their girlfriends if they become pregnant, but others will walk away. I met one young woman, a 21-year-old Russian, who lived with her family in disgrace in a small village outside of Kazan because she had had a child whose father refused to marry her.

The ultimate form of birth control in the former USSR is abortion. Before arriving in the country I had heard appalling statistics about women receiving on average ten to fifteen abortions in a lifetime. The popular newspaper *Komsomolskaia Pravda* reported that 6.5 million abortions took place in the country in 1988—meaning that one of every ten women of childbearing age had one that year. Western researchers have cited even higher figures.

Friends in Kazan confirmed that abortion is a common form of birth control and that it was not unusual for women to have multiple abortions. Women understood that receiving multiple abortions could threaten their capacity to bear children or have other health-threatening effects. As in the West, having an abortion could also be a wrenching emotional experience, though at least women there don't have to contend with anti-abortion protesters outside the doors of their clinics. (There is no anti-abortion movement in the USSR though with the growing desire to emulate the West, there probably soon will be.)

Conditions in Kazan abortion clinics were described as appalling. One woman told me of undergoing an abortion without anesthesia in a room next to a dentist's office, where she could hear the drill whirring in the adjacent room. She lay on an unpadded table, on sheets she herself had been obliged to provide, with little space between her and another woman simultaneously undergoing the same procedure. Soviets could find no privacy even when receiving an abortion.

I once asked a Soviet Ministry of Health official, whom I met at a conference in Moscow, why the country failed to provide more and better contraceptives, thus making a high rate of abortion unavoidable. His response was a dismissive non sequitur: he laughed and asked me how many children I had. He viewed the abortion question as irrelevant.

I got more or less the same response from another Health Ministry official when I asked him about spouse abuse. "We have good husbands in the Soviet Union," he replied, laughing. I did encounter a couple of cases of spouse abuse in the USSR, though my guess, and it's only that, is that it was not as widespread as in the United States.

In general, the Soviet Health Ministry officials reflected the kind of sensitivity toward women's issues that one would anticipate in a country where women are expected to accommodate their menstrual cycle with balls of cotton—if they're fortunate enough even to find them in the stores.

I suppose the Health Ministry officials would have denied the existence of rape, too, but I never got around to asking them about it. Rapes do occur, of course, and there is a great deal of sexual harassment as well, although precise figures, and how they compare with the West, aren't available.

I asked a few people about homosexuality, which was illegal in the Soviet Union (although Yeltsin proposed decriminalization in October 1992), but of course occurs nonetheless. "We have them [homosexuals], but they are not open about their activities" was a typical comment I heard on the subject. Some gays and, even rarer, lesbians have come out of the closet in big cities like Moscow and St. Petersburg, but few are willing to do so in provincial cities such as Kazan.

While it will probably take the former Soviets some time to loosen their taboos against homosexual behavior, pornography has thrived since *glasnost*. In Moscow and other large cities, posters of nudes, sexual horoscopes, how-to and sexual position guides, erotic film shows, and pornographic short stories are sold openly on the streets, in train stations, and undergound metro tunnels. Soviet men and even a few women crowd around the tables, flipping through the pages with rapt attention. In one undergound passage in Moscow I saw a man selling a 1986 *Penthouse* magazine, a real treasure that went for 186 rubles, more than half the average Soviet's monthly salary.

The popular film *Little Vera* broke sexual taboos on screen in the late 1980s and many Soviet cities, including provincial Kazan, regularly featured nude photographic exhibits in downtown galleries. In Kazan on any given day one also could buy *calendari*, baseball card-sized color photographs of nude women with a calendar on the back, which were sold out of kiosks all over town. I was told that erotic and even pornographic videos could be seen in certain porno speakeasies in Kazan, as well as in private homes, reports that I never managed to confirm.

Occasionally a Russian official delivers a blast against pornography and declining moral standards, but my guess is that skin magazines and videos have a real future in the country. There is clearly a market for pornography among men and, besides, as many people reason these days, the West has lots of porn so it must be a good thing.

I'm afraid that AIDS, too, will spread rapidly across the USSR. As of November 1991, there were 700 cases officially confirmed, along with 30 deaths, but the number of unreported cases was thought to be much higher.

Soviets were aware of the dangers of AIDS—the acronym is pronounced *speed* in Russian—but the level of promiscuity and the disdain of condoms represent a real danger for the spread of the fatal disease. Warning posters and educational brochures on AIDS were abundant in 1990–91, but I got the feeling they were ignored along with the exhortations of support for *perestroika* and the ideas of Lenin that appeared alongside them.

Official state warnings against the spread of AIDS seemed somewhat contradictory in view of the thriving flesh trade, which was at least tolerated—and more likely encouraged—by the state in Soviet Intourist hotels. Prostitution, formally illegal in the USSR, brings in millions of dollars, yen, marks, pounds, and lira every year. High-class prostitutes swoop down on foreign currency paying customers in Intourist hotel cash bars like flies at a Georgia picnic. There is probably not an Intourist hotel in the country where a cash-paying customer could not find a "hotel girl" if he wanted one.

Having traveled widely in the USSR, I encountered scores of

prostitutes, from St. Petersburg to Central Asia. I once made the mistake of cashing in a hotel bar a $100 traveler's check—which is, by the way, very hard to do in view of the shortage of dollars in the country. While waiting at the counter I suddenly felt a tap on my shoulder and heard the whisper in my ear: "Vud zyou like to make love?"

I turned around to confront a pair of oversized breasts hanging out of a tight dress that contained a smiling blond-haired woman who was by then pressing her thighs against my leg. I stuttered some kind of negative response and fled on this first encounter, but by the end of the year I was conducting long and engaging conversations with the hotel working women.

The prostitutes I met all catered to foreigners in the Intourist hotels. Cheaper hookers reportedly worked for rubles on the streets, in train stations, and in hotels frequented by Soviets, though I never encountered any of these women. Two kinds of prostitutes worked in the tourist hotels: part-timers who come in three or four times a month, and full-timers who report to work five or six nights a week, often at the same hotel.

I met one of the first variety, a woman named Larisa, who at age 30 was older than most—some "women" begin work at 13 and 14. Larisa approached me as I sipped a beer at the bar in one of Leningrad's finest tourist hotels. She wore an inviting smile and a blouse that revealed a gold chain swaying across a valley of cleavage.

She gave me the "Hi, sailor" routine, but I pleaded that I had just said goodnight to my mother and sister, who were visiting the country for a few days and staying at the hotel, and she could hardly expect me to follow that up by doing business with her. I told her I'd like to talk, however, and would be glad to buy her a drink.

With scores of prostitutes to compete with and business slow because of the decline in tourism, she hadn't given up on me so easily and thus accepted the offer of a drink.

"Can you talk about your work here?" I asked her, explaining that I wanted to write a book about my experiences in the USSR.

"Yes, I can talk, why not?" she said. She explained that she came to the hotel "two or three times" a month to pick up some hard currency to help support her son and her mother. Her husband, she added cheerfully, was a worthless drunk. Larisa insisted that she was "not a professional."

She explained that she had to pay the doorman to enter the hotel, agreeing to leave by a certain time, and also had to give a percentage of her take to the bartender and, if she went up to a room with a customer, to the *dezhurnaia*, the name for the female attendants who sit at desks monitoring events on each floor of the tourist hotels.

"What about the KGB?" I asked, having heard that the Soviet secret police used prostitutes to find things out about foreigners. She waved a hand in dismissal. "The KGB is nothing. It doesn't play any role."

Was she worried about the police? I asked. Larisa laughed derisively and said, "No one cares. They no longer do anything."

"How much do you usually charge?" I asked.

"Well," Larisa responded, "I heard one girl saying $200 tonight, but I can see you are a nice man, so for you—$150."

"No, I really can't," I said.

"I was offered $100 by a Turk just a minute ago," she went on, "but I could tell by looking at him that he was such a type, not for $1,000 would I go with him! I don't like the Finns, either, they are very crude, but you are a nice American," she smiled. "I will go to your room right now for $100."

Heroically, I remained focused on getting information. "Do you use condoms?" I asked.

"It depends on the person," Larisa replied. "It is not too difficult to look at them and tell if they are dangerous. I am healthy and I can see that you are, too," she added. "We don't have to use one and you can kiss me on the mouth. I will make you happy."

I proceeded to lecture Larisa on the dangers of having sex with strange men without using a condom, though she insisted she could tell whether someone had a sexually transmitted disease—the incidence of which is increasing dramatically across the USSR—simply by looking at them.

I told her I had an early plane, which was true, and had to go to bed. I insisted she take $20 for the information she'd given me, an offer she sincerely tried to refuse before I folded the bill into her hand and told her to buy something nice for her son.

We had really liked each other. In fact, I realized after talking to other hotel women, and discarding the usual stereotypical baggage that comes along with the term "prostitute," that I liked most of them. The fact was that, with Soviet society such as it was, many of them were intelligent, even successful women who were the envy, as well as the subject of scorn, of many.

A poll in the magazine *Semia* (Family) found a substantial number of young women considered prostitution a prestigious profession. In another survey, when asked what profession they aspired to, an astonishing 75 percent of teenage girls in Moscow responded "hard currency prostitute."

The reason was not hard to understand. Many of the women, in addition to being very attractive and appearing glamorous, were very well off because of their access to hard currency. The full-time professionals turned over part of their income to Mafia or state sponsors in return for Western fashions, purses, and jewelry that made them the best dressed women in the USSR. They could shop at the foreign currency stores where average citizens couldn't even get in the door. They met interesting foreigners and, quite often, married them as a means of getting out of the country. If they didn't leave permanently, many at least received all-expenses paid trips to Western capitals to serve as mistresses to wealthy foreign businessmen. If nothing else, the hotel girls got to spend their evenings in nice surroundings having their drinks and dinner bought for them. Many of them were friendly with one another, though there was some competition, and spent most of their time in the hotels socializing with each other.

Such a lifestyle compared favorably with the grim lives many Soviets were forced to lead. Getting a little drunk and spending twenty minutes in a hotel room with an older, usually harmless, foreign tourist didn't seem like too high a price to pay, especially for those who learned to manage such liaisons skillfully. In many cases, the hotel women lived at home with their families, who gave them emotional support in their work and shared in the profits. No wonder the ranks of hotel prostitutes are growing: the Moscow, Kiev, and St. Petersburg hotel bars were jammed with working women in 1990–91, far more than I had seen on my first visit to the country in 1987. "Brothels and dens of sin are springing up like mushrooms after rain," complained the head of Moscow's vice squad, the first ever formed, in 1991.

Many of the prostitutes were quite intelligent, diverging sharply from the image of desperate, barely literate streetwalkers wearing heavy facial makeup. Some carried foreign phrase books and learned to speak the requisite number of words in several languages—English, French, German, Italian, even a little Japanese. (One woman told me she preferred Japanese men because they never haggled over price. She branded young American customers as the most obnoxious.)

The growing popularity of prostitution reflects the frustrations many young women anticipate in following traditional sex roles in society. The Soviet Union, like the rest of the world, was a sexist and patriarchal society in which traditional gender roles were clearly defined.

Women are expected to behave in a certain way and perform certain chores and men are expected to play their roles as well. Most women wear makeup and jewelry and dress nicely in skirts, dresses, and stockings, though younger women are starting to dress more casually and be more risqué. Women can drink but are generally expected to be more moderate and often stick to wine rather than vodka. Smoking by women is still frowned upon, at least in provincial Russia, where I had women friends who went behind buildings or stood in stairwells to sneak cigarettes. Women are expected to marry by their early twenties, to prepare all the meals, do the dishes and laundry, clean the apartments, and bear the brunt of the child-rearing.

Men are expected to be the main breadwinner in the family, which places enormous pressures on many of them in an era of inflation and economic collapse. Men can smoke freely, drink all the vodka they want, and don't suffer as much from the *defitsit* in clothing, as fashion is not nearly as important to them. Men are expected to know how to do home repairs, fix the car if they have one, and perform heavy lifting chores. They are expected to play with children and help tote them around, but they don't necessarily have to learn how to change a diaper.

I talked to many Soviets about changing gender roles in the West, explaining that women wanted equal access to jobs and education and equal pay for equal work. I told them about couples where wives expected their husbands to play a more active role in child-rearing and help with food preparation and other domestic chores.

Some Soviet men laughed, shaking their heads in wonder at this appalling prospect, but even many women were troubled by the image of male homemaking.

"It's true that our lives are very hard," observed one woman in Kazan, who both worked and raised children, "but all the same I wouldn't want a husband who did those [domestic] things. That type of man is less than a real man, he is a little bit feminine." Real men don't do housework, she averred.

Women often deferred to men in discussions about the state of society and other weighty matters, although when women spoke up I noticed that their views were not automatically dismissed and were usually accorded legitimacy by Soviet men.

On the other hand I also noticed many examples of sexism, sometimes quite blatant. Even my physicist friend Ildar, a very bright man on most subjects, was a confirmed sexist. "Women will never be as competent as men because they will always be more worried about how they look than anything else," he once told me, as his wife sat nearby with a bemused smile, shaking her head. When I responded that some of the differences were cultural, that women were concerned about their appearance because society pressured women to make themselves attractive to men, Ildar said, "No, that's not it, it is genetic. Women are simply intellectually inferior to men."

Given the sexism, the unequal burden borne by women, and the level of promiscuity, it's no surprise that many marriages end in divorce; the rate in the former USSR is more than one in three. There are still more unhappy marriages that don't end in divorce, largely because the family is deeply valued in Soviet culture and parents strive to keep the family unit intact for the sake of their children.

Family values are as old as mother Russia herself. Parents dote on their children to the point that many Westerners consider Russian children completely spoiled. Many kids are pampered from birth, as symbolized by the practice of swaddling, whereby children are protected from the harsh outdoor environment by being wrapped in layers of clothing and blankets so that none of their skin shows and one wonders how the tiny babies even breathe, entombed as they are in their portable cradles.

Parents are very solicitous of their children, which is why the *defitsit* in children's clothing and playthings is so psychologically devastating. Often at parties children are allowed to climb around, to yell and scream and do as they please while parents and guests give them command of center stage. All these practices are particularly pronounced in single-child families, which are very common because of economic pressures and tight living space.

Soviet parents don't seem to try to regulate, mold, or scold their children as much as in the United States. Rather, it seems, their indulgence reflects an effort to prolong childhood and innocence because they know that their children will confront the grim realities of everyday life soon enough.

Family values always come first—before work, before play, before friendship, before anything. My close friend and translator Leonia once informed me the day before a lecture that he couldn't translate for me the next day because his wife was returning from out of the country and he and the family had to meet her at the train station. Why couldn't he just meet her at home an hour later, after the class?, I wondered, but then realized it was an important symbolic gesture that the whole family reunite at the train station.

Holidays typically are spent together with the family, not with other friends at, say, a New Year's Eve party, as Americans might do. (On the other hand, husbands and wives do commonly go on separate vacations.) I found that many Soviets were appalled at the idea of rest or retirement homes for the elderly, who typically live out their years in three-generation households all over the country.

Family life in the former USSR is not idyllic, of course, and the institution is plagued by various forms of dysfunction. But it is the family, more than anything else, that people cling to in this time of trouble.

CHAPTER ELEVEN

The Long Road Home

❧

IN THE OPENING SCENE of the film *Apocalypse Now*, Capt. Willard (played by Martin Sheen) is seen lying on his sweat-soaked bed, feverish from the heat and staring catatonically at the ceiling fan. He is on the verge of cracking up from too much booze and the hardships of life in a foreign land.

Granted, I hadn't been through anything like the Vietnam War, but eight months in the USSR found me identifying with Sheen's character.

Sometime in May winter had given way to summer in Kazan, spring having been bypassed altogether, and it had become stifling hot in my ninth-floor apartment. There was no fan (much less an air conditioner) to be found in the entire Tatar republic. I kept my screenless windows open at night in quest of cool air, but that merely allowed the mosquitoes from the nearby swamp to flit into my bedroom and torment me through the night.

While not engaged in swatting mosquitoes, I spent those sleepless nights visualizing the simple pleasures of my former existence. I wanted to see family and friends, read the morning newspaper, eat salads made with fresh lettuce, not a leaf of which had I seen in months. I longed to be served by smiling waitpersons in sparkling clean restaurants, watch a baseball game, take a drive in the country—in short, to be a spoiled American once again.

The ominous trend manifested itself one Friday afternoon in early May when I bribed a clerk to get a last-minute ticket on the overnight train for a weekend in Moscow. My sole reason for going was to eat at Pizza Hut and read a copy of *USA Today*.

If I was that eager for pizza and American pop journalism, I concluded that perhaps it was time for me to go home. I made plans to leave the first week of June.

As always during my months in the USSR, nothing turned out as planned. Travel opportunities kept materializing and I couldn't seem to turn them down. Like Capt. Willard, who managed to pull himself together to take up his mission to locate Kurtz in the Cambodian jungles, I would prolong my stay and journey deeper into the disintegrating empire that spanned half the globe.

In fact, I stayed almost two more full months, traveling thousands of miles from St. Petersburg, to Central Asia, across Siberia, and down to the Caucasus. I flew more miles on Aeroflot than most people thought advisable. If the Soviet airline had a frequent flyer program, I certainly would have qualified.

When the second semester finally ended in mid-May, I decided to go on a trip to Soviet Central Asia with my friend Andrea, who went by the name Andy. She was an English teacher from London who worked at an institute in Kazan.

We secured visas and plane tickets to fly to Tashkent, the capital of Uzbekistan, the most populous (more than 20 million) of the five republics that composed the now defunct Soviet Central Asia, which is actually a subcontinent of its own and a place like nowhere else in the rest of the former USSR.

Arriving in Tashkent, we took a cab to our assigned hotel, where we were met by a tall Russian named Boris (pronounced Bahreese), who worked for *Sputnik*, the Soviet youth travel agency. We told the hotel clerk we'd just as soon stay in the same room, rather than share with strangers of the same sex, as was the usual practice in double-occupancy Soviet hotels. The clerk shook her head, giggling, and insisted we'd have to pay for two rooms since Soviet hotels didn't allow unmarried couples to share a room, even if it had two beds. "We have a very moral country," Boris gravely observed .

After I graciously shared with Boris a few curt observations of my own about the state of Soviet morals, we decided to just pay for two rooms. We really didn't mind getting an extra room since they were at least honoring the exchange agreement and letting us pay in rubles, which even many Soviets were now beginning to think of merely as play money.

Finally ensconced, we set out to have a look at Tashkent, a sprawling city of more than a million people and the hub for travelers to Central Asia. Incorporated into the Russian Empire in 1865, Tashkent still reflects its original apartheid character in the sharp divergence between the more modern, russified sections and the sixteenth-century city, where mosques, outdoor markets, sidewalk-sized streets, and a maze of mud and grass huts abound.

Andy and I ambled around the plentiful market, where we stopped to munch on some fresh cherries, before walking to the Barak-Khana Medrese, the headquarters of the Islamic faith in Central Asia. Islam is the predominant religion throughout Central Asia and the Uzbeks, Turkmens, Tadzhiks, Kazakhs, and Kirghizes who adhere to it not only outnumber the Russians by more than two to one, but have a much higher birthrate, all of which helps explain the disintegration of Soviet power in the region.

Passing under a stone arch into the courtyard of the great mosque, we stopped to have a look at men kneeling on prayer rugs spread across a suspended stage. A bearded Uzbek man wearing the traditional black skullcap and a flowing robe approached and demanded to know the reason for our presence. We were just wandering around, we said. "This is not a place to wander around," he shot back, and told us to leave. We obeyed.

That night we caught a bus and then a private car to Tashkent University, where we spent the evening with a friend of another British colleague, an English teacher at the university. The woman, named Bernadette, and her handsome Uzbek boyfriend, for whom she was trying unsuccessfully to obtain a visa to visit England, treated us to drinks and hors d'oeuvres while we watched Western rock music videos on Uzbek television and talked about Uzbek nationalism. Before *perestroika* and *glasnost*, the Uzbeks had been content to blend in with the Russians as the most advantageous route to personal advancement, but thereafter there had been a dramatic resurgence of national pride. "The Russians used to control the Uzbeks," Bernadette observed, "but they're afraid of them now."

The situation mirrored the ethnic tensions that existed between the Tatars and Russians in Kazan and between Russians and other minorities across the USSR. Traveling around Central Asia, it became clear to me that the multi-ethnic Soviet empire was imploding on its periphery.

We received a scare upon arrival the next day in the ancient city of Samarkand, 270 kilometers west, still in Uzbekistan. Our Aeroflot jet landed just before dusk and we hurried out of the terminal to find a taxi. Andy, more fluent in Russian, came to terms with one of the drivers and climbed into the front seat. However, when I opened the back door and started to slide in, a dark-haired Uzbek teenage boy darted in ahead of me.

"Why did you let your woman sit up front?" he asked.

This puzzling question was followed by a series of non sequiturs that were meant to divert my attention while the youth's accomplice slipped his hand into my left front pant pocket, which contained an assortment of rubles, dollars, and, most important, my passport.

Fortunately, the kid was not a professional. When I felt his hand rummaging through my pocket, I yelled and pushed him away. The Uzbek boys seemed offended by my violent reaction, but they were really shocked when Andy erupted, bolting out of the front seat of the taxi and shouting at them at the top of her lungs, "Fuck off, fuck off, just fuck off!"

The Uzbeks seemed to comprehend the meaning of this particular verb, as they backed away from us, now chortling. We got back in the taxi, where the driver, who was probably in on the whole operation, evidenced great amusement about the events that had just transpired. "Had his hand in your pocket, hand in your pocket" he kept repeating in Russian, doubling over with laughter.

Before he pulled out, another man, this one older and more menacing looking than the teenage boys, had replaced the youth in the back seat beside me, which did nothing to calm my frayed nerves. I began to growl like Belker, the undercover cop in the Hill Street Blues television series, in an effort to ward off any additional attacks, but our ride was calm.

When we got to our destination a few minutes later, we met our new *Sputnik* guide, a 25-year-old kid named Mikroch. I angrily recounted what had happened at the airport.

"Welcome to Asia," he said, laughing uproariously. The Uzbeks, I had to conclude, found petty crime highly amusing.

Samarkand itself more than made up for the unsettling incident at the airport. It is a marvelous city filled with stunning medieval architectural masterpieces and resonating the allure of the Orient. I was so overwhelmed by the place that I half expected to see flying carpets whipping across the sky and genies popping out of bottles.

The city contains five building complexes of historic mosques and *medrisi*—medieval colleges promoting religious education— featured blue-tiled domes, minarets, ancient tombs, and sparkling multi-colored colonnades. There is also a medieval observatory, whose fifteenth-century founder, Ulug-Beg, recorded many astronomical observations in advance of Gallileo, who gets all the credit in the West. Ulug-Beg didn't get much respect even in his own time—his scientific observations made the reigning mullahs so nervous they had him assassinated.

The majestic Registan, which alone is worth the trip to Samarkand, dominates the main square of this ancient city. Three massive brick and tile walls surrounded by towers, arches, Persian icons, and minarets enclose the great square. I imagined Alexander the Great, Genghis Khan, and Tamburlaine, all of whom lived in Samarkand at one time or another, appearing high above the square before masses of chanting followers.

As we spent our days strolling through the city's monuments, we noticed that many were adorned with scaffolding, but we rarely saw anyone actually working at historic preservation. On the ground below the walls and towers, fragments of the bright medieval tile were becoming lost forever in piles of rubble, symbolic of the erosion of Soviet authority itself.

Andy and I roamed through the outdoor markets, where occasional blasts of Western heavy metal music erupted from a boom box, overwhelming the creaking sound of traditional Eastern music. We found an outdoor eatery covered by a great canopy to block the scorching heat of the sun, for which Central Asia is notorious. The Uzbek cafe specialized in grilled chicken with a hot sauce, fresh pita bread, and crumbling deep-fried white fish. We ate our main meal there every day, pulling at our food with greasy fingers while turbanned men and women in long-flowing purple and red gowns peered at us from the raised platforms, which looked like four-poster beds, on which they sat, legs crossed, around a foot-high dining table. They looked well-fed and more content than my neighbors back in Kazan.

It was early in the season in a decidedly off-year for tourism and we felt like we had the place to ourselves. The bar in our Intourist hotel was virtually empty—there weren't even any prostitutes. The economic collapse and political uncertainty were keeping most foreigners away. The melancholy barman, who said the place had been full at the same time the year before, couldn't accept my $50 traveler's check—the hotel had no cash to make change.

Outside the hotel I met a young man whom I agreed to try to help out by exchanging hard currency for some of his rubles, in direct violation of Soviet law. He had a friend who'd emigrated to Israel, he explained, and he was saving money so that he might go visit him.

We agreed to meet in a park across the street from the hotel in order to avoid the scrutiny of the KGB functionaries, who spent most of their time grinding out cigarette stubs in their ashtrays in the hotel lobby. I met the 20-something kid at the appointed time, his eyes darting back and forth into the night to see that we weren't being watched.

We both asked each other one last time whether the other one was KGB, and laughed. "It would be five or six years in jail for me, right away," he said, growing serious. I expressed incredulity at the severity of the sentence, but he insisted it was true. We made the exchange and chatted a little while on the park benches. "Thank you for helping me," he said at last. "Hard currency (*valuta*) gives us a chance to travel, which is very important to us what with our extremely boring lives here." We shook hands and parted.

The next day Andy and I left early in the morning for a one-day visit to Bukhara, another ancient city teeming with historic treasures. It was a dusty desert town partitioned by the Ark, a massive but now-crumbling fortress wall that once protected the old city from invasion.

We had risked our lives by spending some seven hours in a speeding taxi getting there and back. Absence of lanes, weaving, tailgating, honking, dodging potholes, speeding, headlights optional at night—these were normal driving practices that anyone familiar with life on the Soviet roads, from Vladivostok to St. Petersburg, simply has to get used to.

But the drivers in Central Asia were something else again.

We whizzed across the arid countryside, past huge, unproductive state farms, on a four-lane highway divided by a concrete wall. We'd come around a turn at 80 and the driver would whip into the next lane, just before obliterating a peasant wagon pulled by a donkey, or a bicyclist, or even a man bumping along on a scraggly camel.

Three or four times we encountered cars and motorcycles coming directly at us at high speeds on *our side* of the divided highway. Having met a few trucks holding up traffic on their side, they had simply cut through a break in the divided highway to drive on our side for a while. Our taxi driver shook his head nervously after one near miss. "Soviet power no longer extends out here," he explained, "so people now do as they please on the roads."

We were happy to be alive when we arrived back in Samarkand that night and happier still when we landed back "home" in Kazan the next day. I had only a day to recover from Central Asia, however, before boarding another Aeroflot jet for St. Petersburg, where I was to meet my mother and sister who had decided to visit the USSR while I was there. They had been on a typical, week-long Intourist tour of Moscow and St. Petersburg, where I met them in one of that city's finer hotels.

My mother, who'd spent the whole year reading about Soviet food shortages and worrying about her son, greeted me with an explosion of tears and both she and my sister expressed shock at my supposedly emaciated condition, though I felt better without the twenty pounds I'd shed.

It was a spectacular time to be in St. Petersburg, which is one of the most beautiful cities in Europe any season, but is even more special during *Belye nochi*, the white nights, when darkness never settles in the high latitudes over the canals, drawbridges, stunning architectural monuments, and the warren of backstreets that once haunted Dostoyevsky. The city's modern residents, the most radical anti-communists in the USSR, were abuzz over the upcoming referendum in which they voted to change the name of the city from Leningrad back to the pre-revolutionary St. Petersburg. The Soviet government refused to honor the referendum until the aftermath of the failed August coup, whereupon the name was immediately changed.

I once again found it strange, after having lived like a Soviet for most of the year, to join my mother and sister in their comfortable tourist hotel. I ate with them and their small tour group under gilded chandeliers in the white tablecloth dining room. But even here in the artificial world of Intourist the realities of Soviet society filtered through. Our waiters spent more time using their broken English to hawk tins of caviar, concealed under their white towels, along with amber necklaces, all part of the relentless quest for hard currency. My mother and sister encountered a young Soviet woman who sequestered herself in a hotel restroom to avoid the authorities as she tried to sell the tourist women jewelry as they came in. Other women, of course, were openly selling their bodies in the hotel's three foreign currency bars. At the Hermitage, the glorious historic displays of Russian culture inside gave way to crowds of children and teenagers besieging foreigners for their hard currency as they stepped off their tourist buses outside. The *fartsofchiki*—currency speculators, or people who trade or sell with foreigners—lurked all across the great cobbled square where eighty-five years before the tsar's palace guard ignited the first phase of the Russian Revolution by firing on a crowd of protesters on "Bloody Sunday."

I enjoyed spending time with my mother and sister but after a few days I needed to get away from the tourist scene. I had the address of a Kazan friend named Gulia, who was studying for a year in St. Petersburg, and decided to go see her.

She had no phone so I simply showed up at her dormitory. Not really expecting to find her, I tactlessly brought nothing, not even flowers, but Gulia received me with a big smile, summoned her friends, and a party promptly materialized. As we gathered around a stool in a tiny dorm room, someone brought a couple of bottles of vodka and a few morsels of food, what little they had on hand, and Yugoslav cigarettes. We drank toasts, laughed, played a popular card game called *Durak*, or Fool, that distinction going to the last player stuck holding cards. I'd honed my skills, having been the *durak* many times before when I'd first played the game in Kazan, and survived several hands without being the fool.

We all collapsed into our respective narrow dorm beds, even as light streamed through the windows at 3 A.M. I had been warmed by yet another display of spontaneous Soviet hospitality and simple humanity, a welcome change from the pervasive groveling that had enveloped the tourist sites.

The next day, my last in St. Petersburg, I had to find a way to get out of the city. By June, a large number of Soviets and foreigners were traveling, especially in the western USSR, and I couldn't obtain a train ticket to Moscow and then on to Kazan. However, my mother's tour guide, a fiftyish career Intourist employee named Marina, who was also leaving that day, said she could find me a plane ticket to Kazan.

I accompanied Marina, my mother, sister, and the rest of their group to the St. Petersburg airport for their flight to Helsinki and then on to New York. My mother erupted in tears again, as we kissed good-bye at the gate, leaving me in a melancholy mood. "Mothers are the same all over the world," observed Marina, patting me on the shoulder as we waved farewell.

I spent the next couple of hours with Marina, whom I found to be one of a vanishing breed of Soviets, a true believer in both socialism and the Russian empire. We both agreed that we hated to see the citizenry selling themselves and groveling for dollars, rejecting in their desperation those things that were good about Soviet life in a naïve faith that the Western model had all the answers to their problems.

"I don't know what is wrong with our people," Marina observed in her fine English. "I see them chasing all of you Americans around for your dollars and I am ashamed for my country."

Marina herself refused to take tips in hard currency from her foreign visitors, though they were readily offered to her and in amounts that would have made her quite wealthy by Soviet standards. Most Intourist guides were not nearly as principled.

No mere reactionary in the mold of those who attempted the August coup, Marina, a Russian, respected Gorbachev and the changes he had tried to effect, though she admitted that his "economic policies are not good. They are not working. . . . I simply don't know what will become of us," she sighed, shaking her head.

After seeing off my mother's tour group at the international wing, we caught a taxi to the other side of the airport. The driver turned out to be a dark, balding Azerbaijani who, without prompting, began to excoriate the Soviet government. He said that his brother had died in the violence at Nogorno-Karabakh, a disputed Armenian enclave, senselessly created inside Azerbaijani borders by Stalin. "My mother was not even allowed to put flowers on the grave," the driver continued, his voice rising, "that's the kind of country we live in."

"Can't you at least try to get along with each other?" asked Marina, in reference to the ethnic violence between Armenians and Azerbaijanis.

"Who needs to get along with those people [Armenians]," the driver shot back. "There will be war!"

"You see," said Marina, turning to me in the back seat, "our people don't even want to try to get along. I can't understand what is happening to us," she added, shaking her head.

By the time I returned to Kazan, exhausted from my travels to Central Asia and St. Petersburg, I was determined to pack my things and book a flight home, only to be confronted by the offer of yet another journey into the unknown. I discovered that my friend Doog, the British linguist, and I had been invited on a *kommande-rovka*, a Soviet business trip—to Siberia. He was to give a couple of lectures for English teachers at a technical institute in Krasnoyarsk, in west-central Siberia, and I would give one on higher education in the United States.

We took an overnight flight, across the Urals and the *taiga* (an endless sub-arctic forest) to Krasnoyarsk, a city of about one million on the Yenisey River, one of the many wide streams flowing from the Arctic glaciers, down through the northern tundra, before emptying in Lake Baikal. The modern Krasnoyarsk, rebuilt after an 1873 fire wiped out the old city, was now a transport center and the site of sensitive refrigeration and satellite industries that had left the city closed to foreign visitors until December 1990.

Doog and I were among only a handful of Westerners ever to visit the place.

We were met at the airport by a couple of instructors from the institute and some local businessmen, who took us to a relatively modern hotel, where we were allowed to catch up on sleep. We gave our talks the next day before enthusiastic audiences at the rundown technical institute, where faded wall posters attested to the blessings of *perestroika* and chipped marble busts of Marx, Engels, and Lenin abounded.

We spent only a few hours actually working before settling in for three days of intense socializing, all of which made ours a typical Soviet "business trip." Our hosts gave us an auto tour of the city, which included a stop at a modern riverfront complex, adjacent to the obligatory Lenin Museum—as always, the nicest, and least patronized, building in the city. Many more people soon would be attending a new building under construction nearby— a Seventh Day Adventist church. We learned fun facts such as that Peace Street used to be called Stalin Street and that the "American football" team in town called itself the Siberian Bears.

Doog and I found Krasnoyarsk to be mellower and more provincial than the Western cities we were familiar with. The populace, predominantly Russian, dressed more conservatively and conducted their lives at a more relaxed pace, but the Siberians were no less hostile to Soviet authority than their brethren across the disintegrating union. Only sugar had to be rationed here, but the food stores were as empty as anywhere else and the proletariat in an angry mood. "There, that's what communism has given us," one of our escorts, Nikolai, commented bitterly as we passed a long line outside a food store in the city center.

Most, though not all, of our hosts were decidedly anti-Soviet. Nikolai, who said he had rejected the party line since the early 1960s, was particularly vituperative. "Look at how repressive North Korea is," he averred. "That's the logical result of communism. All of the communists are criminals who have made our lives miserable."

Despite his claim to misery, Nikolai had a roomy apartment, a charming wife, and two teenage children, who grilled me over dinner about the names and relative popularity of Western rock groups and sports teams. Nikolai himself was eager to make contact with Western businessmen and asked me if I could refer some of them to him. He wanted to promote tourism along the Yenisey and said he could arrange for the sale of some of Siberia's abundant natural resources in exchange for hard currency. "Help us sell our forest," he offered, waving off our environmental protestations. "Ah, we've got plenty of trees."

Our lack of business contacts left Nikolai disappointed, but he and his family, as well as the instructors from the institute, continued to entertain us in grand Russian style. We drove around the countryside outside the city, visiting a massive hydroelectric dam the state had built to electrify the whole Krasnoyarsk region. We hiked through a pine forest to the *Stolbee*, prominent rock formations overlooking the Yenisey and a favored site for Soviet alpinists. Each night we were feted with huge meals and, as always, an ample supply of vodka, which found us reeling, on our last night, onto a

3 A.M. train bound for Irkutsk. We waved good-bye to yet another group of people whom we had never met before but who had touched us with their boundless supplies of warmth and generosity.

After an eighteen-hour haul on the famed trans-Siberian railroad, Doog and I arrived in Irkutsk, where we were met by another of his language teacher colleagues from the British Council. We had now come literally thousands of miles aboard plane and train, across the mountains, steppes, and *taiga*—and were still only halfway across endless Siberia.

Irkutsk, a beautiful and historic city of half a million residents, was developed by the aristocratic rebels, the Decembrists, who had failed in their attempt to topple the tsar in 1825. As punishment for their treason, which, incidentally, inspired young Lenin when he read about it years later, the tsar sentenced the Decembrists to permanent Siberian exile, with many of them settling in Irkutsk. The exiled aristocrats built the finest schools, hospitals, and cultural facilities in Siberia, a tradition that has been maintained along with the neo-classical wooden homes that appear throughout the city.

While three hundred thirty-six streams flow into nearby Lake Baikal, only the Angara River, which flows through Irkutsk, flows *out* of the lake, its point of departure marked by a huge crag jutting out of the water in mid-stream. This geographical oddity gave rise to a wonderful legend among the local Buriat people, which held that Angara, Old Man Baikal's beautiful daughter, refused the marriage her father had arranged for her with the Irkut River. Defying her father on a moonlit night, she broke out to be united with the far-off Yenisey, a handsome dark stranger with whom she had fallen in love. Awakened in the night by her departure, the enraged Baikal hurled a giant rock, the crag that now marks the point of departure, but failed to stop his daughter from breaking away.

Baikal is indeed the stuff of legends. There is simply no other place like it. The size of Belgium, it is the largest, deepest (1.6 kilometers), and cleanest freshwater lake in the world, home to 1,200 living species that are unique to Baikal.

I joined Doog and some friends as we took a train that wound through the pine forest up and down the shore of Lake Baikal. We got off not far from the Buriat Autonomous Republic, which borders on Mongolia, and set off into the woods for an overnight camp-out. We had a fine time hiking in, then wading into an icy cold Siberian river by our campsite, cooking over an open fire, and fighting off mosquitoes the size of condors before crawling into our tents for the night.

As we returned to Irkutsk and prepared to head back across the Urals, Doog and I reflected that the Siberians we'd met were un-mistakably Russian in character, though more laid back and further removed from the divisive political issues that dominated discussion in Moscow, St. Petersburg, and even Kazan. Many of the Easterners we met, especially around Baikal, loved the outdoors and were ea-ger to promote tourism in the region as a means of accessing hard currency.

We took another all-night flight—the lumbering Aeroflot jet, overloaded, seeming to barely get off the ground—and headed back across several time zones to Kazan. When we stopped in Novosi-birsk for refueling, the men climbed off the plane to stretch their legs and smoke cigarettes on the tarmac, casually flicking their ashes while a truck pumped jet fuel only a few meters away.

Back in Kazan, I began at last to prepare to leave the country once and for all when Andy, my Central Asian traveling partner, prevailed upon me to take still one more trip—this time to the Cau-casus. "Look at it this way," she cajoled, not wanting to travel alone, "if you got to Tbilisi on top of everything else, you will have seen it all and will never have to come back here again."

I was subject to temptation because I had heard many Soviet friends rank Georgia, along with Central Asia and the Crimea, as the most interesting places to visit in the USSR. The fact that the Georgians had already made it clear that they no longer considered themselves part of the Soviet Union and that an incipient civil war was going on in the republic were, we ultimately decided, insuffi-cient reasons to stay away.

I did decide to continue westward, toward home, after our visit to the Caucasus, which meant that the time had come to say good-bye to Kazan.

My emotions were mixed, but intense. I'd been in Kazan long enough that some of my friends had come to consider me part of the environment and I often felt the same way. I had evolved all sorts of relationships of varying intensity with all manner of differ-ent people—older and younger, male and female, intellectual and working class. Now that I had learned my way around, I had even, in fleeting moments, imagined what it would be like to stay, semipermanently, to take the going native approach to its logical extreme. But those thoughts *had* been fleeting.

In some ways I was quite eager to get out of Kazan, to leave behind my stifling hot apartment, the bad memories of my failed relationship with Tania, the still awkward encounters with my History Department colleagues. On the other hand, I had grown quite close to a number of people, especially Leonia, Doog, Ildar, Galina, and scores of others with whom I'd enjoyed many good times, but now had to say good-bye to, perhaps forever. There were more of these obligations than I could possibly meet in an appropriate way, but I did the best I could with a series of farewell dinners and last cups of tea. Some of these occasions, as with the last supper with Leonia and his family, became quite somber as the finality of the situation settled upon us.

When the day of departure came, Andy and I caught a taxi from the university, where ten or twelve of my closest friends gathered under the gigantic portrait of Lenin in the main hall, for last good-byes and a farewell photograph.

And then I was gone from Kazan.

Arriving in Tbilisi via Aeroflot, we rendezvoused at the airport with some Georgian acquaintances of Leonia, only to discover that my bulging internal frame backpack, stuffed with my last possessions after I had given away most of my stuff to friends in Kazan, was nowhere to be found. When everyone else had removed their bags from the conveyor, I went behind an "employees only" door and demanded to know where my bag was.

The worker who'd unloaded the bags claimed he had no clue. When I continued to demand answers, he took me back out across the tarmac to the jet we had flown in on. I placed one foot into his locked hands and he hoisted me up for a look inside the cargo bin, but there was nothing there. We went to the other side and climbed up the ramp on board to see if anyone there knew where my bag was, but only a co-pilot, filling out a flight report, remained.

I was angry now, convinced that my luggage had been stolen and not lost. "Does this kind of thing happen often?" I snapped at the Aeroflot co-pilot.

"Whadda you think," he sneered in response, "it's the Soviet Union isn't it?"

By the time I returned to the terminal, the Georgians who had met us had gotten in on the act and began to question top airport administrators, in Georgian. I don't know what they said, but it was something to the effect that this was a terrible embarrassment and no way to treat a visiting professor from America, and so on.

I filled out a lost baggage form and left the airport, convinced that I would never again see my camera, shortwave radio, and even more valuable notes and photographs. What a fool I had been to have let that bag out of my sight!

We arrived at a Georgian home a half hour later and were being treated to a late-night supper when the phone rang and the airport officials announced they had "found" my bag. I got up early the next morning and caught a taxi out to the airport to retrieve it. Had it not been for our new Georgian friends, I would never have seen my things again. Although no one could explain what happened, everything was intact, though the bag had been rummaged.

That crisis averted, we settled in for three full days in Tbilisi, which means "warm springs" in Georgian. Armenia, Azerbaijan, and Georgia composed the three Caucasian republics, which had already effectively broken from Soviet control.

The watershed event as far as the Georgians were concerned came on April 9, 1989, the night of the "massacre" in which Soviet troops killed twenty protesters in downtown Tbilisi, allegedly even bludgeoning a grandmother to death as she tried to crawl away. Flowers and a memorial gravestone marked the site of the violence in the city center, just down the street from the former Institute of Marxism-Leninism, now renamed the rather more prosaic Institute of Political Study.

The Tbilisi massacre, like "Bloody Sunday" in Vilnius, the Lithuanian capital, in January 1991, was a desperate thrust by the regime against the steady erosion of Soviet power. "After the massacre we really understood the nature of the system we were confronting," one of our hosts told us. "After that there was no going back [as part of the USSR]."

Months later, in the fall of 1990, the Georgian independence drive culminated when an angry throng pulled down the giant statue of Lenin, precipitating a night of fireworks and celebration. Lenin Square was renamed Freedom Square and today contains only grass and no monument. The Georgians subsequently overwhelmingly elected a new president, Zviad Gamsakhurdia, an intensely nationalistic and authoritarian ruler who had once been jailed by Soviet authorities. Following my own return home to the United States, I sat stunned before my television as it depicted scenes of violent conflict taking place on the streets I'd strolled only weeks before. The virtual civil war resulted in Gamsakhurdia's ouster, though the situation in Georgia remains unstable.

At the time of our visit to Georgia, however, the populace was so preoccupied with hating the Soviets that they hadn't gotten around yet to turning on each other. Many Georgians we spoke with were convinced that Moscow had instituted an economic blockade against them in response to the drive for independence, leaving their store shelves barren and almost all basic foods available, if at all, only through rationing. One man, a Georgian with characteristic jet-black hair and sharp features, told me he hadn't seen butter in a year. "Now it is possible to exist," he observed, "but not to live."

During our visit, Soviet troops occupied parts of Georgia, including south Ossetia, an autonomous republic inside Georgia whose residents, predominantly ethnic Ossetians, wanted to be reunited with north Ossetia—located inside the neighboring Russian Republic. Most Ossetians, in other words, wanted no part of an independent Georgia. Gamsakhurdia, insisting that South Ossetia was part of Georgia, revoked the republic's autonomous status and the region has subsequently been plagued by protracted violence.

As Andy and I toured and discussed these issues with our new acquaintances, they more than confirmed Georgia's reputation for boundless hospitality. They mobilized all their resources to ensure that we ate like royalty: wonderful fresh salads, hot eggplant dishes, fresh baked breads with cheeses melted in the middle, cakes for dessert, and bottle after bottle of sweet Georgian wine, of which there was no *defitsit*. "Drink, drink, drink," our hosts would tell me, filling my glass. "It is not unusual for our men to drink three bottles of wine with dinner."

When not being compelled to eat and drink, we meandered around Tbilisi, a city of more than a million, divided in half by the muddy River Kura, which flows into the Caspian Sea. We dipped in and out of the myriad shops, museums, and cafes, none of which struck us as the least bit Soviet. Aided by a favorable climate, Georgia has always been more bountiful and prosperous, enjoying a higher standard of living and higher per capita car ownership than the rest of the Soviet republics. The architecture, large wooden houses with roomy apartments and wide verandas, was like nothing we'd seen elsewhere in the USSR. The Georgian language and culture, dating as far back as the twelfth century B.C., added to the place's uniqueness. We could see why the Georgians didn't consider themselves part of the USSR and that they would never be brought back without violence and indefinite military occupation.

Filled with national pride, Georgians will reel off the names of famous countrymen, although they grow hesitant when the name of the most famous Georgian of all—Stalin—comes to the surface. Although Stalin personally authorized the liquidation of millions of Soviets during the collectivization of the 1930s, many Georgians (as well as many Soviets) prefer to believe, as one told us, that Stalin "just continued what Lenin started. He is not the most guilty."

Some Georgians are openly apologetic for the brutal Soviet dictator. Andy and I decided to take another long taxi drive, from Tbilisi to Gori, Stalin's birthplace, where his defenders are legion. Our driver, a Gori native, told us that Stalin was a great leader because "when he was in power we had everything."

"What about the millions of people he killed?" Andy shot back, but the driver just shrugged, as if the issue didn't concern him.

We arrived in Gori, a squalid little town with nothing whatsoever of interest aside from the last remaining Stalin statue in the former USSR, which towers imperiously over the main square. A tiny mud and brick cabin, in which Stalin spent his childhood, has been preserved nearby, but the great stone Stalin museum, with its marble floors and a grand hallway and staircase, has been closed to visitors for three years, since Stalin's crimes were widely exposed under *glasnost*.

We returned from Gori and spent a last night with our Georgian hosts in Tbilisi before Andy and I said our good-byes, as she headed back to Kazan and I on to Odessa. I had no friends or contacts in Odessa, but simply had decided to spend a last couple of days collecting myself on the Black Sea coast before leaving for home.

Once I had flown over the Black Sea and into Odessa, I could see why Russians are so fond of the place. A bustling port city, it has an exciting, cosmopolitan flavor that has become part of Russian folklore since the writings of Pushkin, whom the tsar exiled to the city in the 1820s.

As always, my plans—in this case, I had envisioned a couple of days' relaxation on the beach—had to be scuttled. When I made my way to the seacoast, a thin layer of chemical soot coated the sea surface and signs warned of the hazards of going into the water. The place smelled like the Love Canal. Once one of the most desirable beach resorts in the country, Odessa had become a toxic waste dump.

After two days in Odessa, I was more than ready to leave the USSR behind, but when I inquired at Aeroflot I found that I couldn't fly out of the country from Odessa, even though it was closer to the West. I had no choice but to return to Moscow. How could I have forgotten that everything went through Moscow in the old USSR? That is, after all, one of the main reasons it no longer exists.

Though accustomed to the absurdities of Soviet life, I was still feeling put out until I met a Turkish businessman who regularly commuted to Odessa. Although Istanbul is located just across the Black Sea from Odessa, my Turkish friend explained that on each of the many trips he made every year, he had to fly hundreds of miles out of his way to Moscow. Only then did Soviet authorities allow him to go on to Odessa.

After waiting a routine couple of hours in line, I learned that Aeroflot wouldn't sell me a ticket to Moscow for rubles, regardless of what my exchange agreement mandated. At that point I didn't really care, I just wanted to leave the country any way I could, so I handed over my credit card without even putting up an argument. The Soviet bureaucracy finally had beaten me down.

Sorry, the Aeroflot clerk said, handing my Visa card back, she wasn't authorized to accept credit cards. Okay, I said, taking out two $50 traveler's checks to cover the $99 cost of the ticket, take these, and keep the change. Nope, she said, eyeing the checks, can't take those either, cash only please.

I patiently explained that I didn't carry around $100 in cash, adding that traveler's checks were the same as cash. The clerk looked the checks over again, but wouldn't buy it. She advised me to go the main Aeroflot office at the airport and see what I could work out there.

At this point I began to think that I, like Pushkin, would be trapped in Odessa for a long period of exile. I thought I'd think more clearly about the situation over a beer at the hotel bar and ended up discussing my predicament with a boat pilot, a Russian named Kolia, who was paying for his drinks in marks that he'd picked up on his last voyage. As I'd seen happen so often before when I described my experiences in the USSR, he cringed with embarrassment over my account of the difficulties caused by the Soviet bureaucracy, and offered to go with me to the airport. "All you need to do," he said, "is slip $20 inside your passport when you hand it over to the clerk and she will sell you a ticket for rubles and keep the *valuta* for herself."

Sounds good to me, I said, and off we went to the airport. When I attempted this gambit, however, the clerk refused to take the money and handed back my passport, shaking her head. "With a Russian she would have done it right away," Kolia explained, "but with foreigners they are still a little nervous about the KGB." The man behind us in line, another Russian named Sasha, overheard Kolia and I pleading with the clerk and exploded with rage.

"What are you doing!" he roared, pushing between us and pressing his face into the glass that divided him from the Aeroflot clerk. "This American only wants to buy a ticket to Moscow," he roared. "What kind of country do we have where he cannot even buy a plane ticket?" By this time Sasha's face was turning red and eyes blazed, as scores of heads turned to witness the public scene. "I am sick of this horrible shit in our country," he went on. "*Sell this man a ticket right now!!*"

An Aeroflot administrator quickly materialized from an interior office and motioned us behind closed doors. Sasha, who, it had become clear, had had a few drinks that night, berated her and the entire Soviet state, while Kolia and I quietly waited to see if it would do any good. Sasha and the Aeroflot administrator argued back and forth for several minutes before she finally looked over my visa and exchange agreement and agreed to sell me a ticket for rubles for the 8 A.M. flight to Moscow.

Arrangements made, I left the airport on a bus with my two new Soviet friends. I shook hands and said goodbye to Kolia, as he got out at his stop. When Sasha hopped out at his a few moments later, he promised to meet me the next morning at the airport terminal to make sure everything was all right. "You don't have to do that," I said, "it's after midnight and you've already arranged everything."

"No," he said, "I will be there because they have probably lied to us. They lie to us all of the time, you see." Despite his words, I fully expected Sasha to be sleeping off his hangover, but there he was the next morning, waiting for me at 7 A.M. We shook hands, went in, and bought the ticket for rubles, just as promised. Before he saw me off, I insisted that Sasha take the $20 with which I had originally planned to bribe the Aeroflot clerk. The offer insulted him—he had helped me out of friendship and embarrassment about the state of his country—but at the same time I knew that he could use the hard currency. I insisted that he take it and, in the end, he did.

As Sasha, the last of hundreds of warm-hearted Soviet friends I had met by chance, waved good-bye, I boarded an Aeroflot jet bound for Moscow. I spent two days sleeping in a Moscow tourist hotel before climbing aboard a 747, operated by the soon-to-be-defunct Pan American Airlines, for a final flight out of the soon-to-be-defunct Union of Soviet Socialist Republics.

As my taxi pulled into Sheremetievo International Airport, where my Soviet journey had begun ten months before, I was over-whelmed with emotion. Before entering the terminal, I carried my bag around a corner of the building.

And cried.

Epilogue

❧

I HAD BARELY BEGUN to recover and make sense of my life back home amid the glorious comforts of Western civilization when the August 19, 1991, attempted coup in Moscow erupted like a great volcano, spewing uncertainty in every direction.

Even though I had spent ten months living in provincial Russia and trooping around the USSR, I suddenly realized that I no more than anyone else could predict with any assurance the ultimate outcome of the attempted *putsch*.

Soviet President Mikhail Gorbachev had wanted to effect sweeping reform, but got revolution instead. Out of touch for too long behind the high Kremlin walls, Mikhail Sergeyevich did not comprehend until it was far too late the depth of anger and despair rumbling beneath the surface of Soviet society. Had he lived for a few days like an ordinary Russian or Tatar in Kazan, he might have done better, though in the final analysis the USSR probably was a patient that was beyond saving. Nonetheless, to his everlasting credit, Gorbachev did not opt for attempts at repression, which undoubtedly would have been both bloody and futile.

Americans, with their usual proclivity for oversimplification and putting themselves at the center of all world events, promptly pronounced that the disintegration of Soviet and East European communism marked the worldwide triumph of American values. Invoking Woodrow Wilson's vision of a world made "safe for democracy," as well as Henry Luce's notion that the twentieth was to be the "American century," President George Bush declared that the end of the cold war, in combination with the pummelling of Iraq, signaled the triumph of a "new world order" constructed on liberal capitalist lines.

The academic community weighed in with books arguing that the United States was "bound to lead" and one previously unknown State Department functionary, Francis Fukuyama, even went so far as to declare that the global triumph of American-style liberalism represented "the end of history." According to Fukuyama, the human spirit yearns for something akin to liberal democracy and, now that such ideas have triumphed in the former communist world, we are at the end of history, or at least that part of it devoted to revealing the proper paradigm for governing human affairs.

We shall see about all of this. Although I am skeptical about grandiose claims with respect to the universality of American or even Western values, I do find myself more receptive than I would have thought possible before my experience in the former USSR. After spending ten months observing Soviet society "from the bottom up," it did become clear to me that, in certain fundamental respects, the West had indeed conquered the East. As their own system disintegrated, millions of former Soviets looked to Western-style capitalism for salvation. Even before the coup, popular discourse—not only in Moscow and St. Petersburg, but also in provincial regions such as Kazan—centered on transition to a market economy and joint ventures with Western capitalists, all of it accompanied by a profusion of advertising, from billboards to radio and television.

Western, and especially Hollywood films, television series, and rock videos also underlay the triumph of the Western model. I once sat for four hours in a packed theater watching *Gone With the Wind*, which absolutely enraptured a Soviet audience that could relate to the romanticized, downtrodden South. The fact that a single male voiceover did Rhett as well as Scarlett (to say nothing of Mammy) didn't bother them at all. *Gone With the Wind* is a classic, but *Elvira, Mistress of the Dark*? My Soviet friends loved that, too, and virtually all the American films, even the tacky R-rated ones that rolled into the city each week. I learned that Johnny Weismueller's Tarzan films had been shown on Soviet TV when all the kids in my apartment complex spent the rest of the afternoon swinging on the monkey bars in the courtyard below, screaming "Aaahhheeeeeahhh," like the venerable ape man himself, as I myself had done as a boy. Rock videos, reruns of "The Muppet Show" and "Dallas" and many others also captivated Soviet households.

While all this may appear perfectly harmless, I'm not so sure. Many of the people I met during the course of my stay in the former USSR—and especially the younger generation—derived their images of life in the West from these sources. Many seemed to believe that if only they lived in an individualistic society, they could excel, be rich, enjoy a big, comfortable home, wear the latest makeup and fashions, have fast private cars and beautiful boyfriends and girlfriends with hard bodies and happy Hollywood smiles. When I tried to suggest that some of this Hollywood fluff might be alienating, that these images created false expectations and eroded community in favor of individual aggrandizement, that some valuable aspects of Russian culture might be lost in the transition, they scoffed at me and offered to trade places and become Americans themselves. If I liked the Soviet Union so much, I could stay. Their motto seemed to be "Russia: hate it and try to leave it."

Most former Soviets have had little real exposure to capitalist society. Rarely did I meet a Soviet who had stopped to think that some day he or she might actually have to pay a real rent on the apartment long provided by the state for a nominal sum each month. Some looked horrified when I told them that when people in the West found it difficult to find affordable housing, the state couldn't be counted on to help them, that we had a growing army of homeless. Many people failed to work hard in old USSR, to be sure, but all were at least guaranteed some sort of a job, and that no longer prevails.

For the longest time embittered Soviets could blame the Communist regime for all their woes, and of course it did fail them. But now that it is gone, they are left with a deepening economic and social crisis but no all-encompassing center of evil on which to place the blame. "Now we don't even know what country we live in," one of my correspondents wrote in the fall of 1992. "The USSR has passed away but we still live with the passports of a nonexistent country and according to its laws."

"We have freedom now," wrote another of my friends, "but we don't know what to do with it—to steal, to cheat, or to enjoy it. It's not based on anything. . . . People *are* hungry."

Thus, after an initial euphoria over the collapse of communism, people have begun to confront the realities of spiraling inflation and the continuing disintegration of legal, political, and social authority as they attempt the unprecedented conversion from a Communist Party dictatorship to a capitalist mixed economy. Frustration will continue to mount, perhaps to intolerable levels, as state subsidies for food and housing disappear, prices skyrocket, and crime increases. Most of the people I met during my year in Russia already had been beaten down; they bore the collective weight of a century marked by war, revolution, famine, brutal political tumult, and ultimately stagnation and disintegration. It is hard, in the wake of all that, to fashion an upbeat, can-do mentality.

"I am becoming more and more scared for my family, and my [two] children," one Kazan resident wrote to Alsue, my friend who now lives in the northeastern United States. "Prices are increasing, houses are not being built, and the word 'unemployment' now is becoming not only the 'wild western' privilege, but ours also." Another friend began a letter to Alsue by observing that "you should consider this letter as the message from the hell of a living people."

As the situation in Russia continues to deteriorate, we in the West must be prepared for the possibility of further convulsions. It does not appear, as I write in the fall of 1992, that Russia and the other republics have yet hit bottom. Civil war, which has already erupted all around the former Soviet periphery, has not and I hope will not have reason to infect Russia and the other large republics. In "Tatarstan," my correspondents relate, ethnic tensions are palpable but so far have produced only a few relatively minor incidents. In Tataria, "everything is quiet so far," wrote a friend in the fall of 1992.

All of this leaves me in a melancholy mood when I think of life in Russia. I have many fond memories, but I fear for the future of the people I met and for a culture I came to know. As my skills in Russian wane from inattention and the demands of life in the rush-rush USA mount, I have become a poor correspondent. It is also difficult to get a phone call through to Kazan. I do hope to bring Leonia for a long visit to the United States, the country that has always fascinated him, but there is a mountain of bureaucratic and financial obstacles.

As for myself, perhaps I will return to Russia at some point to rethink all this, to check in with my friends, and undertake additional research on East-West relations, especially in this realm of the transference and exchange of culture and its implications. In my mind's eye I can see myself flying into Sheremetievo International Airport and visiting my favorite spots in Moscow before boarding the "Tatarstan" train for the overnight trip to Kazan. There, no matter how devastating the *defitsit*, I'm sure I'll find myself eating huge, leisurely meals interspersed with shots of vodka, laughing, listening to their bitter complaints and speaking in my crude Russian with Leonia and Luda, Ildar and Gulia, Guselle, Assia and Anton and their new baby, with Maia and Farrida too, as well as Galina and all of my other friends at the university. And I'll meet new ones, for it is easy to do over there, especially for an American. Perhaps I'll travel some more, to the now independent Baltic states, which I didn't get to before, or deeper into Siberia, maybe all the way to Vladivostok or even Kamchatka.

Maybe, just maybe, I'll go back and once again put up with the dirt and the grime, the rude bureaucrats and inefficient clerks and all the disorder and mind-boggling contradiction that is Russia.

But if I do, rest assured, I won't be staying for ten months.

Glossary

apparatchik   Communist Party functionary
babushka   grandmother
bania   steambath
Belye Nochi   the "White Nights" (St. Petersburg)
berioza   leaves taken from supposedly medicinal branches of the birch
        tree; used during steambaths
blat   influence, or "pull"
calendar   baseball card-sized color photographs of nude women with a
        calendar on the reverse side
chas pik   rush hour
crizis   crisis
defitsit   shortage, deficit
dezhurnaia   female attendant posted on each floor of Soviet tourist hotels
durak   fool
dusha   spirit, or soul
fartsofchik   currency speculators; persons who trade or sell with
        foreigners
forma   school uniforms
glasnost   openness, free expression
gopnik   a hoodlum, or street criminal
Goskomobrazovanie   the state Education Committee of the USSR
gruppirovki   group, or gang, members
guliat'   to "take a stroll," or to "step out" on a marriage
khitrye   calculating, tricky
khuligani   hooligans
kolbasa   sausage sold in long rolls; a staple of the Soviet diet
kolkhoz   collective farm
kommanderovka   a Soviet business trip
Komsomol   the Communist Youth League
Komsomolskaia Pravda   a popular national newspaper
koshmar   a nightmare

kulak   a wealthy peasant
lubovnik   a lover
militsiia   the police
na levo   on the left, or on the side, or "under the table," as in black market activity
negre   negro
neudobna   uncomfortable, inappropriate for the occasion
nichevo   nothing
nocil'shchik   baggage porter
nomenklatura   power elite
obed   dinner
perestroika   restructuring
pivo   beer
plastinki   records, record albums
prekrasno   wonderful
propiska   official authorization to live and work in a specific Soviet city
rynok   private market
samizdat   underground literature or recordings
"Sayscha"   USA
shashlik   grilled meat on a skewer, shish ka-bob
Sovetskaia Ploshchad   Soviet Square
stakan   drinking glass
staraia devka   an "old maid"
stol   table
stydno   shame, ashamed
tabakanist   tobacco store
taksist   taxi driver
ukaz   official decree
Universityetskaia   the University Hotel (Moscow)
uzhas   horrible
valuta   hard currency
vinovat   guilty
Vremia   "The Times," national television news program
Vzglad   "Viewpoint," a popular television "news magazine" program
yolka   New Year's tree